Routledge Revivals

Where is Britain Going?

First Published in 1926, *Where is Britain Going?* focuses on the historical factors and circumstances which were to define Britain's development in the midst of social unrest at that time. The book considers the future of Britain in an age when the working classes were being driven into confrontation with the state under the impact of the world crisis of capitalism. Writing over eighty years ago, Trotsky concentrates on the decline of British imperialism in his analysis of the Bolshevik Revolution. In a brilliant polemic that exposes all the treachery of the Labour leaders in the year before the General strike, he recalls the revolutionary traditions of the working class and draws on the historical lessons of the English Civil War and Chartism. Rejecting the parliamentary road and stripping bare the pretensions of Fabian socialism, *Where is Britain going?* outlines perspectives of revolution which continue to retain their validity.

Where is Britain Going?

L. Trotsky

Routledge
Taylor & Francis Group

First published in 1926
by George Allen & Unwin Ltd

This edition first published in 2012 by Routledge
2 Park Square, Milton Park, Abingdon, Oxon, OX14 4RN

Simultaneously published in the USA and Canada
by Routledge
711 Third Avenue, New York, NY 10017

Routledge is an imprint of the Taylor & Francis Group, an informa business

ISBN 13: 978-0-415-62340-7 (hbk)
ISBN 13: 978-0-203-10288-6 (ebk)

WHERE IS BRITAIN GOING?

BY

L TROTSKY

With an Introduction by

H. N. BRAILSFORD

LONDON: GEORGE ALLEN & UNWIN LTD.
RUSKIN HOUSE, 40 MUSEUM STREET, W.C. 1

Printed in Great Britain by
UNWIN BROTHERS, LIMITED, LONDON AND WOKING
First Published in 1926

INTRODUCTION

At the close of the Communist trial the judge at the Old Bailey summoned seven of his prisoners to choose between a six months' sentence and the opinions expressed in this book. They are, if we must read this summons in its literal meaning, prohibited opinions on which the law has put its ban. If this were really our case, then the thesis which Trotsky maintains in these pages is established already. For we should have to admit that even before violence had been attempted, the mere appearance in our politics of a tiny revolutionary party has sufficed to frighten the ruling class out of its respect for the liberty of opinion on which democracy is founded. It needs no energetic exercise of the imagination to predict from this episode what would happen if the challenge grew to a formidable threat.

But the battle for freedom is not yet lost. It is precisely those of us who differ from Trotsky's reading of our inevitable destiny who are bound in duty to welcome the appearance of this book. If it may come freely from the press, if it may be discussed, as it deserves to be, with equal freedom for assent or dissent, then, for the moment at least, the nightmare of this trial is dissipated. Of all parties in Great Britain, the Labour Party has the chief interest in demanding for this ruthless attack upon itself both liberty and attention. We can hold our faith in the democratic approach to Socialism as a reasoned conviction only if the opposite opinion may be argued in perfect liberty, and only then if it finds worthy and capable advocates. If the law forbids a man to draw from the study of history and the survey of contemporary politics the conclusion that force is the only adequate instrument for social change, in that moment our contrary opinion ceases to be a reasoned conviction and becomes an imposed dogma.

The opinion which Trotsky maintains has never been more brilliantly argued. Behind its wit and its logic there is the prestige of experience. The pamphleteer who tells us that if we mean to achieve Socialism we cannot escape civil war has himself conducted a civil war against terrific odds to a triumphant conclusion. It is obvious, moreover, that he has taken pains to equip himself for his task and has applied his versatile intellect to the study of our history and our contemporary life. He makes some mistakes,[1] it is true, in his facts, but none of these really invalidate his argument.

His book is a slashing attack on our whole movement. We shall make a grave mistake if we allow its manner to blind us to the fact that he has a strong case to argue. He assails Left and Right with equal vehemence. Sometimes in his criticisms of persons he is arrogant and offensive; sometimes his wit is irresistible; sometimes (it seems to me) he assails things in our record and muddles in our thinking which deserve to be assailed. But the odds are that with these ruthless Russian methods he will produce in the minds of most English readers an effect which is far from his intention.

[1] He evidently misunderstands our electoral system. Again, the life of the Independent Labour Party has been much longer than he supposes, and its membership is twice what he attributes to it. He seems at times to identify it with the Fabian Society. But such slips are of no importance.

Trotsky is far too able a man not to realise that there are differences in the English and Russian national characters. He emphasises again and again the lesson that history has made each of us what we are. Yet the more he displays his acquaintance with the external facts of our history, the less does he seem to understand us. His attitude to the religious beliefs of most of our readers is for me the test of his failure to understand us—and this I may say calmly, since I am myself an Agnostic. No Russian that I ever met, even when he had been long in England, ever grasped the fact that English religion with its long tradition of open discussion, the democratic form of its " free " churches, its emphasis on conduct rather than ritual or belief, and its relative freedom from other worldliness, has literally nothing in common with the Eastern Church. I wonder, would Trotsky's conviction that Protestant religion is necessarily a " bourgeois " creed which no worker can honestly profess survive a visit to a dissenting chapel in a mining district ? Has he ever read Bunyan, or glanced at the revolutionary history of Anti-Baptists and Fifth Monarchy men ? What would he make of the queer disputes between the middle-class Free-thinker, Robert Owen (who hated class war), and the pioneers of English Trade Unionism, who clung with equal obstinacy to their Christianity and their belief in the class war ?

One feels the same failure of a man from another world to understand us when Trotsky laughs at the idea that a Labour majority in Parliament will ever be allowed to do anything fundamental. Assuredly it will be a tremendous adventure ; certainly it will want will and courage. No sane man will deny the risks to which Trotsky points. But equally, I think, every man who realises how deeply the Parliamentary tradition and the instinct of obedience to the majority are graven on the English mind will admit that the adventure is worth attempting. Not only in Parliament, but in churches, Trade Unions, and even clubs, this respect for the majority has been inculcated on generations of Englishmen. What can a Russian know of that? What estimate can he make of the power of tradition in our older civilization? We should answer, in the last resort, that if he is right, if the propertied class will in the end defend its privileges by force, then we prefer to fight, as Cromwell fought, with the Parliament behind us, and the rights of a majority on our side.

But it is not the business of an introducer to enter into controversy with the author. The book with all its vitality and assurance is doubly valuable—as a revelation of the Russian mind, and a criticism of our English ways. It is the work of a shrewd and realistic intellect. It will not convert many of us to the Russian standpoint. But we shall fail to use it to the full unless we take it as a challenge that forces us to think out our position anew. Trotsky sees, as some of us do not, the difficulty of our unparalleled enterprise. He realises that the tactics which will avail to transform an old society cannot be the tactics of an opportunist Liberalism. The book may confirm us in our resolve by all means to avoid civil war, but it is a formidable challenge to us to test our own sincerity, and to ask ourselves whether, with a will and a courage that equal the audacity of these Russian pioneers, we are moving with single minds towards the achievement of our goal.

H. N. BRAILSFORD.

CONTENTS

PREFACE

BRITAIN stands to-day at the turn of the road—much more, indeed, than any other capitalist country. And a change of direction for Britain is in large measure a change of direction for four-fifths of the world, and at least the beginning of a change for the fifth part, to-day the most powerful—America. At the same time the political development of Britain presents great distinctive features of its own, resulting from all her past history and in large measure standing athwart her future path. Without encumbering our exposition with facts and figures, which the reader can easily find for himself in books of reference or in special investigations into Britain's economic situation, we have set ourselves the task of selecting and characterising those historical factors and circumstances which must define Britain's development in the immediate future.

It has to be borne in mind that we shall be talking particularly of Britain, and not of the British Empire, of the mother country, and not of the colonies and dominions. The latter have their own lines of development, which increasingly diverge from the lines followed by the mother country.

Our exposition will be mainly critical and polemical. History is made by people. The evaluation of the vital forces making present-day history cannot but be active in its aspect. In order to understand what the classes, parties, and their leaders are struggling for and what is awaiting them to-morrow, we must tear our way through the dense wall of political conventions, lies, and hypocrisy, and the all-pervading parliamentary "cant."[1] In such a case the polemical becomes the indispensable method of political analysis. But the question which we have set ourselves, and to which we shall endeavour to provide the answer, has an objective character : " Where is Britain going ? "

[1] *Cant.* A specific form of conventional lie, tacitly acknowledged by all through considerations of social hypocrisy. According to Carlyle, cant is the art "whereby a man speaks openly what he does *not* mean." In parliamentary-Protestant Britain this art has been carried to extraordinary heights—or depths.

WHERE IS BRITAIN GOING?

I

THE DECLINE OF BRITAIN

THE way was prepared for capitalist Britain by the political revolution in the middle of the seventeenth century and the so-called industrial revolution at the end of the eighteenth century. Britain emerged from the period of her civil war and the dictatorship of Cromwell as a small nation, hardly numbering 1½ million families. She entered the imperialist war of 1914 as an empire counting within her borders a fifth part of all humanity.

The British revolution of the seventeenth century, the school of Puritanism, the harsh school of Cromwell, —these prepared the British nation, in particular its middle classes, for their further world rôle. From the middle of the eighteenth century Britain's world power had become indubitable. Britain ruled the ocean and created the world market in the process.

In 1826 a certain British Conservative publicist depicted the age of industry in the following terms: "The age which now discloses itself to our view promises to be the age of industry. . . . By industry alliances shall be dictated and national friendships shall be formed. . . . The prospects which are now opening to England almost exceed the boundaries of thought; and can be measured by no standard found in history. . . . The manufacturing industry of England may be fairly computed as four times greater than that of all the other continents taken collectively, and sixteen such continents as Europe could not manufacture so much cotton as England does. . . ." (*Quarterly Review*, June to August, 1826, pp. 92–99.) [1] Great Britain's colossal industrial preponderance over the rest of Europe and over all the world laid the foundations of her wealth and her absolutely unrivalled world position. The age of industry was at the same time the age of Britain's world hegemony.

During the period 1850 to 1880 Britain became the industrial school of Europe and America. But by this very fact her own monopolistic position was undermined. From the eighties onward an obvious weakening of Britain set in. New States entered the world arena, Germany being in the front rank. At the same time Britain's capitalistic primogeniture first began to reveal its detrimental, conservative aspects. Under the heavy blows of German competition the doctrine of free trade wore thin.

The displacement of Great Britain from the position of world domination occupied by her thus came to be openly revealed during the fourth quarter of the last century; and towards the beginning of the present century it produced a state of internal want of confidence and a ferment among the upper classes, and a profound molecular process of an essentially revolutionary character among the working class. Chief place in these processes was occupied by mighty conflicts between labour and capital. It was not only the aristocratic position of British industry in the world, but also the privileged position of the workers' aristocracy in Britain, that was being shaken. The

[1] Max Beer, *A History of British Socialism*, vol. i, p. 283. (Bell, 1921.)

years 1911 to 1913 were times of unparalleled class struggles of the miners, railwaymen, and transport workers generally. In August 1911 a national, in other words a general, strike broke out on the railways. The vague shadow of revolution hovered over Britain in those days. The leaders exerted all their strength in order to paralyse the movement. Their motive was "patriotism"; the affair was occurring at the time of the Agadir incident, which threatened to lead to a war with Germany. As is well known to-day, the Premier summoned the workers' leaders to a secret council, and called them to the salvation of the fatherland. And the leaders did all that lay in their power, strengthening the bourgeoisie, and thus preparing the way for the imperialist slaughter.

The war of 1914–1918 seemed to cut short the revolutionary process. It put a stop to the development of the strike struggle. By leading to the break-up of Germany, it seemed that it had returned to Britain her rôle of world hegemony. But it was quickly revealed that Britain's decline, temporarily checked, had in actuality only been deepened by the war.

In the years 1917 to 1920 the British Labour Movement again passed through an extremely stormy period. Strikes were on the grand scale. MacDonald signed manifestoes from which he to-day recoils in horror. Only after 1920 did the movement return within bounds, after "Black Friday," when the triple alliance of miners', railwaymen's, and transport leaders betrayed the general strike. Paralysed in the sphere of economic action, the energy of the masses was directed on to the political plane. The Labour Party grew out of all expectation.

In what does the change in the external and internal situation of Britain consist?

The gigantic economic preponderance of the United States was developed and revealed during the war in its fullness and completeness. The emergence of the United States from the status of overseas provincialism at once thrust Great Britain into a secondary position.

The "co-operation" of America and Great Britain is the momentarily peaceful form in which Britain's increasing capitulation to America will take place.

This "co-operation" may at this or that moment be directed against a third Power; none the less, the fundamental antagonism of the world is that between Britain and America, and all other antagonisms, severer at a given moment and more immediately threatening, can be understood and evaluated only on the basis of the antagonism between Britain and America.

Anglo-American "co-operation" is preparing the way for a war just as a period of reform prepares for a period of revolution. Just the very fact that, in taking the way of "reforms," i.e. compulsory accommodations with America, Britain will abandon one position after another, must ultimately compel her to offer resistance.

Great Britain's productive forces, and most of all her living productive forces—the proletariat—no longer correspond to the position she holds in the world market. Hence the chronic unemployment.

The commercial and industrial, and the military and naval hegemony of Britain has in the past almost automatically safeguarded the bonds between the various parts of the empire. Even at the end of the last century the Minister of New Zealand, Reeves, wrote: "Two things maintain the present relations between the colonies and England: (1) their belief that England's policy is in the main a policy of peace, and (2) their belief that Britain rules the waves." The decisive factor was, of course, the second condition. The loss of hegemony of the seas goes on parallel with the development of centrifugal force within the empire. The maintenance of imperial unity is continually rendered more difficult by the diverging interests of the dominions and the struggle of the colonies.

The development of military technique proved to be a blow at the immunity of Great Britain. The growth of aviation and means of chemical warfare is rendering valueless the tremendous historical advantages of her island situation. America, that gigantic island guarded on both sides by oceans, remains invulnerable. On the other hand, the most populated centres of Great Britain, and especially London, can in the course of a few hours be subjected to a murderous air attack from the European continent.

Having lost the advantage provided by an inaccessible isolation, the British Government is compelled to participate more and more directly in purely European matters and in European military agreements. Britain's overseas territories, her dominions, have not the least interest in this policy. They are interested in the Pacific, the Indian Ocean, and partly in the Atlantic, but not under any circumstances in the Channel. At the first clash on a world scale this divergence of interests will be transformed into a yawning abyss, in which the imperial bond will be snapped. In the foreknowledge of this, Great Britain is paralysed by internal friction, is doomed in its essence to a policy of passivity, and consequently to a worsening of the world position of the empire.

Meantime, expenditure for war purposes must absorb a continually increasing share of Great Britain's decreasing national revenue.

One of the conditions of Britain's "co-operation" with America is the payment of the gigantic British debt to America, without any hope of her ever receiving payment of the debts owed to her by the continental States. As a result the relationships of economic power will change still further in favour of America.

On March 5th of this year the Bank of England raised the bank rate from 4 to 5 per cent., following the example of the New York Federal Reserve Bank, which had raised its rate from 3 to 3½ per cent. In London the City felt very seriously this sharp reminder of their financial dependence on their cousins from the other side of the Atlantic. But what were they to do? The American gold reserve is approximately 900 million pounds, while the British reserve does not exceed 150 million pounds, or six times less. America has a gold currency, while Great Britain can only make despairing efforts to get back to it. It is natural that, when the rate is raised from 3 to 3½ per cent. in America, Britain should be compelled to answer by a raising of her rate from 4 to 5 per cent. Such a measure strikes a blow at British commerce and industry, by raising the cost of indispensable necessities. In this way at every step America shows Britain her place: in the one case by resorting to diplomatic pressure, in the other by measures of a financial nature; always and everywhere by the pressure of her colossal economic predominance.[1]

[1] Since this was written the British Ministry has adopted a series of measures of a legislative and banking and financial character to safeguard the transfer to a gold currency. Here we seem to have a "great victory" of British capitalism. In actuality, Britain's decline is demonstrated by nothing more clearly than by this financial achievement. Great Britain was compelled to carry out this expensive operation through the pressure of the American dollar standing at par and the financial policy of her own dominions,

Meantime the British Press notes with fear the "striking progress" of various sections of German industry, and in particular of German ship construction. Arising out of the latter, *The Times* of March 10th wrote: "It is probable that one of the factors which makes for the ability of the German yards to compete is the complete 'trustification' of material, from the mine to the fitted plate, from the financing bank to the sale of tickets. This system is not without its effect on wages and the cost of living. When all

which were orientating more and more towards the dollar, turning their backs on the pound sterling. Britain was not able to complete the last step towards a gold currency without the extensive financial "aid" of the United States. But that means that the fate of the pound sterling is directly dependent on New York. The United States is taking into its own hands the mighty weapon of financial repression. Britain is being compelled to pay for this dependence with a high rate of interest. In order to hinder the export of her own gold she is being compelled to undermine the export of her own goods. Meantime she cannot refuse to make the transfer to gold currency without hastening her own decline in the world market of capital. This fatal combination of circumstances evokes a feeling of severe indisposition among the British ruling classes, and causes the growth of a sullen but impotent grumbling in the Conservative Press itself. The *Daily Mail* writes: "By accepting the gold basis the British Government is giving the Federal Bank (which in practice is under the influence of the United States Government) the *possibility of creating a monetary crisis in Britain at any moment it chooses.* The British Government is bringing the whole financial policy of its own country into subjection to a foreign nation. . . . The British Empire is being mortgaged to the United States." "Thanks to Churchill," writes the Conservative newspaper the *Daily Express*, "Britain is falling under the heel of the American bankers." The *Daily Chronicle* expresses itself still more decidedly: "Britain is in fact degraded to the position of being the forty-ninth State of America." It is impossible to speak more clearly and expressively! To all these severe self-reproaches (without inferences or perspectives as they are) the Chancellor of the Exchequer, Churchill, answers in the sense that there is nothing else for Britain to do other than bring her financial system into conformity with reality. Churchill's words signify: we have become immeasurably poorer, the United States immeasurably richer; we must either enter into a struggle with her, or subjugate ourselves to her; in placing the future of the pound sterling in dependence on the American bankers we simply translate our general economic decline into terms of currency; we cannot jump over our own heads; we must "conform with reality."

these forces are turned into the same direction the margin for reduction in costs becomes very considerable." In other words, *The Times* here declares that the organic superiority of the more up-to-date German industry will again be revealed in all its might as soon as Germany is afforded the possibility of displaying signs of life externally.

There are, it is true, indications that the order for ships was placed with the Hamburg yard for the special purpose of frightening the trade unions and thus preparing the ground for bringing pressure to bear on them with a view to lowering wages and lengthening the hours of labour. Needless to say, that manœuvre is more than likely. But that does not in the least weaken the force of our general considerations on the irrational organisation of British industry and on the overhead expenses arising out of that organisation.

It is now four years since the number of officially registered unemployed in Britain fell below 1,135,000, and in fact it has oscillated between 1¼ and 1½ millions. This chronic unemployment is the most clamant disclosure of the insolvency of the regime; it is its Achilles heel. The Unemployed Insurance Bill introduced in 1920 was framed to meet exceptional circumstances, which were quickly to pass. But unemployment became permanent, and insurance ceased to be insurance; the contributions of the interested persons were quite inadequate to cover the payments made to the unemployed. The British unemployed are no longer to be regarded as a "normal" reserve army, now decreasing and now increasing, and continually renewing the elements of its composition, but a kind of permanent social stratum created by industry during the period of expansion and rejected by it in the period of depression. This is a gouty growth in the social organism, a morbid change of tissue.

The President of the Federation of British Industries, Colonel Willey, declared at the beginning of April that the receipts from industrial capital during the last two years have been so insignificant that they could not stimulate the entrepreneurs to a development of industry. Enterprises do not give any higher percentages than paper values with fixed interest (State loans and so on). "Our national problem is not a problem of production but a problem of markets." But how can you resolve the problem of markets? It is necessary to produce more cheaply than do others. Yet in order to do this it is necessary either radically to reorganise industry, or to lower taxation, or to cut down workers' wages, or to combine all these three methods. The cutting down of wages, which can give only an insignificant result in the sense of lowering the cost of production, arouses strenuous opposition, for the workers are even now struggling for a rise in wages. It is not possible to lower taxation once it has become necessary to pay debts, to establish a gold currency, to maintain the apparatus of empire—yes, and to maintain 1½ million unemployed in addition. All these items are charged to the cost of production. Industry could be reorganised only by putting fresh capital into it. Meanwhile the small profits compel free capital to be put into State and other loans.

Stanley Machin, the President of the Association of British Chambers of Commerce, at this same time declared that the solution to the unemployment problem was emigration. The amiable fatherland tells the million or so of hardworking men—who, together with their families, make up several million citizens: "Stuff yourselves in the hold and be off somewhere or other overseas!" The complete bankruptcy of the capitalist regime is herein confessed without any circumlocution.

We must consider the internal life of Britain from the perspective outlined above of a sharp and continually increasing decline of the world rôle of Great Britain, which country, while still retaining the whole of her possessions, apparatus, and the tradition of world domination, is in actuality being more and more thrust into the position of a second-rate Power.

The break-up of the Liberal Party is the consummation of a hundred years of development of capitalist economy and bourgeois society. The loss of world hegemony has left whole branches of industry in a blind alley and has struck a mortal blow at the independent industrial and commercial capital of medium size—that which is the basis of Liberalism. Free trade has come to an impasse.

Meantime the stability of the capitalist regime has been in large measure diminished by the division of labour and of authority between Conservatism and Liberalism. The break-up of Liberalism discloses all the other inconsistencies in the world position of bourgeois Britain, and at the same time reveals the source of the internal instability of the regime. The Labour Party in its upper circles is very akin politically to the Liberals, but it is not capable of restoring its former stability to British parliamentarism, since the Labour Party is itself only a brief stage in the revolutionary development of the working class. MacDonald has a still shakier seat than has Lloyd George.

In the beginning of the fifties Marx estimated that the Conservative Party would quickly pass from the scene, and that all political developments would follow the line of a struggle between Liberalism and Socialism. This forecast postulated a quick tempo to revolutionary development in Britain and Europe. Just as, for example, our Kadet Party (Constitutional Democrats) under the pressure of the revolution became the sole party of the landowners and the bourgeoisie, so British Liberalism would have absorbed the Conservative Party, becoming the sole party of property, if during the course of the second half of the nineteenth century a revolutionary attack by the proletariat had developed. But Marx's prophecy was made right on the eve of a new epoch of sudden capitalistic development (1851–1873). Chartism finally disappeared. The workers' movement went the way of trade unionism. The ruling classes obtained the possibility of outwardly masking their inconsistencies in the form of a struggle between the Liberal and the Conservative Parties. By rocking the parliamentary swing from right to left and from left to right, the bourgeoisie found a vent for the opposition sentiment of the working masses.

German competition was the first threatening warning to the British world hegemony and struck it the first serious blow. Freedom of trade came up against the superiority of German technique and organisation. British Liberalism was only the political generalisation of Free Trade. From the time of the bourgeois-cum-property electoral reform of 1832 and the repeal of the Corn Laws in 1846 the Manchester school occupied a dominating position. For the course of the next half-century the doctrine of free trade seemed an immutable programme. In conformity with this the directing rôle belonged to the Liberals, and the workers followed at their tail. From the middle of the seventies a hitch occurred in affairs.

Free Trade was discredited and the protectionist movement set in. The bourgeoisie were captured more and more by imperialist tendencies. Symptoms of the decomposition of the Liberal Party were revealed even in Gladstone's time, when a group of Liberals and Radicals with Chamberlain at their head raised the standard of protectionism and joined forces with the Conservatives. From the middle of the nineties commercial affairs took a turn for the better. This delayed Britain's political transformation. But towards the beginning of the twentieth century Liberalism, as the party of the middle classes, was seen to be breaking up. Its leader, Rosebery, openly ranged himself beneath the standard of imperialism. However, the Liberal Party was fated to pass once more through a period of expansion before it disappeared from the scene. Under the influence of the manifest decline of British capital's hegemony on the one hand, and of the mighty revolutionary movement on the other, there developed a political awakening of the working class, and the latter, applying itself to the creation of a Parliamentary Labour Party, was at first as a flood to the mill of Liberal opposition. In 1906 Liberalism came again to office. But by its very nature this expansion could not last for long. The political line of the proletariat led to the further growth of the Labour Party. Before 1906 the representation of the Labour Party grew more or less in accordance with the Liberal representation. After 1906 the Labour Party began to grow obviously at the expense of the Liberals.

Formally it was the Liberals, through Lloyd George, who led the way in the war. In actuality the imperialist war, from which the sacred regime of Free Trade did not save Britain, could not but inevitably strengthen the Conservatives as being the most consistent party of imperialism. Thus the final touches were given to the preparations for the Labour Party's entrance on the scene.

While impotently dallying around the problem of unemployment, the Labour Party daily, the *Daily Herald*, draws from the capitalist avowals above quoted the general conclusions that, since the British capitalists prefer giving money loans to foreign Governments rather than to industrial expansion, there remains nothing for the British workers to do except carry on without the capitalists. The conclusion, speaking broadly, is correct, but it is deduced not at all in order to stir up the workers to chase out the capitalists, but only to urge the capitalists along the road of "progressive efforts." As we see, all the policy of the Labour Party hangs on this. For this the Webbs write a whole book, MacDonald delivers speeches, the editors of the *Daily Herald* put out daily leading articles. Meantime, if these miserable attempts to frighten the capitalists are successful, it is in the completely contrary direction. Every serious British bourgeois understands that behind the theatrical threats of the Labour Party leaders is hidden a very real danger from the profoundly disquieted proletarian masses. It is just because of this that the wise bourgeoisie draws the conclusion that it is better not to sink fresh resources in industry.

The bourgeois dread of revolution is not always and under all conditions a "progressive" factor. Thus there can be no doubt that British economy would gain great benefits from the co-operation of Britain with Russia. But this presupposes a great plan, large credits, and the adaptation of an important part of British industry to the needs of Russia. The obstacle to this is the bourgeois fear of revolution, the lack of confidence in to-morrow shown by the capitalists.

The dread of revolution drove the British capitalists along the road of concessions and reorganisation, so long as the British bourgeoisie, thanks to their world position, retained gigantic resources of manœuvring in their own hands. They could legalise trade unions, repeal the Corn Laws, raise wages, extend the electoral law, institute social reforms, and so forth. But in Britain's present radically changed world position the threat of revolution has no longer force to drive the bourgeoisie forward; on the contrary, it paralyses the last remnants of their industrial initiative. What is necessary now is not the threat of revolution, but the revolution itself.

The above enumerated factors and circumstances do not any of them possess an accidental and transient character. They develop in one and the same direction, systematically worsening Great Britain's international and internal situation, and giving to it the character of being without historic issue.

The contradictions undermining Britain's social organism will inevitably intensify. We do not intend to prophesy what will be the tempo of this process, but in any case it will be measured in terms of years, or at the utmost in terms of five years, not at all by decades. The general prospect is such that it is necessary first of all to ask oneself the question: Will a Communist Party have time to grow up in Britain, sufficiently strong, sufficiently linked with the masses, to draw at the necessary moment all the indispensable practical conclusions from the intensifying crisis? In this question Great Britain's destiny is to-day summed up.

II

MR. BALDWIN AND . . . GRADUALNESS

On March 12th of the present year Mr. Baldwin, the British Prime Minister and leader of the Conservative Party, delivered a long speech on the destiny of Britain to a Conservative audience at Leeds. This speech, like many other of Mr. Baldwin's outbursts, was pervaded with an anxious tone. We consider that from the point of view of Mr. Baldwin's party this anxiety is completely justified. We ourselves shall approach these same questions from a somewhat different angle. Mr. Baldwin is afraid of Socialism, and in his demonstrations of the danger and difficulty of the road to Socialism Mr. Baldwin made a somewhat unexpected attempt to find support in the author of this book. That gives us, we hope, the right to answer Mr. Baldwin without risk of being accused of interfering in the internal affairs of Great Britain.

Mr. Baldwin considers, and not without reason, that the greatest danger to the regime which he supports is the growth of the Labour Party. Of course, he hopes for victory, since " our (the Conservatives') principles are in closer accord with the character and conditions of our people than any traditions or principles of violent change." None the less, the Conservative leader reminds his audience that the last election verdict of the country was not final. Mr. Baldwin himself knows infallibly, of course, that Socialism is not practicable. But since he is in a somewhat confused state of mind, and since, in addition, he was speaking to an audience which even without this was convinced of the impracticability of Socialism, Mr. Baldwin's conclusions along this line were not distinguished by their originality. He reminded the Conservative audience that children are born neither free, nor equal, nor fraternal. He turned to every mother at the meeting with the question: Were her children born equal? The smug and uncavilling smirk of the audience was his answer. True, the mass of the British people heard the same arguments from the spiritual great-great-grandfathers of Mr. Baldwin in answer to their demand for the right of freedom of belief and to be allowed to set up their church after their own fashion. These same arguments were afterwards adduced against equality before a court, and later, even quite recently, against universal suffrage. People are not born equal, Mr. Baldwin; why then do they have to answer before one and the same court, according to one and the same law? One could have replied to Mr. Baldwin that although children are not born all alike, yet the mother customarily feeds her dissimilar children alike at the table, and takes care, if she is able, to ensure that they shall all have a pair of shoes on their feet. A bad stepmother acts in a different fashion. One could have explained to Mr. Baldwin that Socialism is not at all concerned with the creation of an anatomical, physiological, and psychical equality, but endeavours only to ensure to all people similar material conditions of existence. But we will not trouble our readers with the further development of these very elementary ideas. Mr. Baldwin himself, if he is interested, can turn to suitable sources, and since by the nature of his world outlook he is more disposed to the old and purely British authors, we may recommend to him Robert Owen, who it is true had no understanding whatever of the class dynamics of capitalist society, but in whose works one can find most valuable considerations on the advantages of Socialism.

But it goes without saying that the Socialist aim, in itself sufficiently reprehensible, does not frighten Mr. Baldwin so much as the violent road to it. Mr. Baldwin notes two tendencies in the Labour Party. One of them is represented, according to him, by Mr. Sidney Webb, who recognised the " inevitability of gradualness." But, according to his own words, there is another kind of leader, such as Cook or Wheatley, especially since the latter relinquished his ministerial post, who believes in force. According to Mr. Baldwin, Government responsibility, generally speaking, had a salutary action on the leaders of the Labour Party and compelled them to recognise with Webb the unsuitability of revolutionary methods and the advantages of gradualness. At this point Mr. Baldwin intervened in a kind of spiritual fashion in Russian affairs, in order to enrich his own far from rich arsenal of evidence against British Socialism.

We quote verbatim from *The Times* report:

" The Prime Minister quoted Trotsky, who, he said, had discovered in the last few years and written ' that the more easily did the Russian proletariat pass through the revolutionary crisis, the harder becomes now its constructive work.' Trotsky had also said what no leader of the extremists had yet said in England: ' We must learn to work more efficiently.' He wondered how many votes would be cast for a revolution in England if people were told that the only (?) result would be that they would have to work more efficiently. (Laughter and cheers.) Trotsky said in his book: 'In Russia, before and after the revolution, there existed and exists unchanged Russian human nature.' (?) Trotsky, the man of action, studied realities. He had slowly and reluctantly discovered what Mr. Webb discovered two years ago—'the inevitability of gradualness.'" (Laughter and cheers.)

Of course, it is very flattering to be recommended to a Conservative audience at Leeds: more a mortal can scarcely desire. It is almost as flattering to be brought into immediate association with Mr. Sidney Webb, the prophet of gradualness. But before we can accept this honour we have a mind to obtain certain authoritative explanations from Mr. Baldwin.

It never entered the heads either of our teachers or of ourselves, even before the experience of "these last few years," to deny the gradualness of development either in nature or in human society, its economy, politics, or morals. We would desire only to make certain stipulations concerning the character of this gradualness. Thus, taking an example dear to Mr. Baldwin as a Protectionist, we appeal to the fact that Germany, having during the fourth quarter of the last century entered the arena of world competition, became an extraordinarily dangerous competitor of Great Britain. As is well known, it was in this way that the war came. Does Baldwin regard the war as a manifestation of methods of gradualness? During the war the Conservative Party demanded the "destruction of the Huns" and the overthrow of the German Kaiser by the might of the British sword. From the point of view of the theory of gradualness, it would surely have been more correct to rely on the elevation of German morality and the gradual betterment of her mutual relations with Britain. However, during the years 1914–1918 Mr. Baldwin, so far as we remember, categorically denied the applicability of the method of gradualness to Anglo-German relationships, and endeavoured to decide the question with the aid of the greatest quantities of explosive material possible. We suggest that dynamite and lignite can hardly be recognised as instruments of conservative-evolutionary action.

Pre-war Germany, in her turn, did not arise in her armed might from the sea-foam in a morning. No, she developed gradually from the basis of her previous economic insignificance. Thus, the wars that Prussia waged, in 1864 with Denmark, in 1866 with Austria, and in 1870 with France, played a colossal rôle in the expansion of her might, and afforded her the possibility of entering triumphantly into world competition with Britain.

Wealth, which is the result of human labour, is without doubt built up with a certain gradualness. But perhaps Mr. Baldwin will agree to recognise that the war years caused a gigantic bound upwards in the wealth of the United States. The gradualness of accumulation was greatly modified by the war catastrophe, which caused an impoverishment of Europe and a frenzied enrichment of America.

Of the jumps in his own personal experience, Mr. Baldwin spoke in his parliamentary speech devoted to trade unions. In his youth Mr. Baldwin directed a factory which had been handed down from generation to generation, where the workers were born and died, and where in consequence the principle of patriarchal gradualness ruled in its completeness. But a miners' strike broke out, the factory could not work owing to lack of coal, and Mr. Baldwin was compelled to close it down and let the thousand of " his own " workers disperse to the four corners of the earth. True, Mr. Baldwin may plead the bad will of the miners, who compelled him to break a sacred Conservative principle. The miners doubtless could appeal to the lack of good will of their patrons, who compelled them to enter on a great strike, causing a break in the monotonous process of exploitation. But in the last resort the subjective impulses are a matter of indifference ; for us it is enough that gradualness in various spheres of life goes on side by side with catastrophes, ruptures, and leaps forward and backward. The long process of competition between two States *gradually* prepares the way for war, the dissatisfaction of exploited workers *gradually* prepares the way for a strike, the bad management of a bank *gradually* prepares the way for bankruptcy.

The worthy Conservative leader may say, truly, that war and bankruptcy, the impoverishment of Europe and the enrichment of America at her expense, are all very sad, and that generally speaking it would be better to avoid them. We have nothing to answer to this beyond saying that the history of nations is in large part the history of wars, and the history of economic development is embellished with statistics of bankruptcy. Mr. Baldwin, doubtless, would say at this point that that is a peculiarity of human nature. Granted that it is so, but that in itself signifies that the very " nature " of humanity combines in itself gradual development and catastrophic change.

However, the history of humanity is not only the history of wars, but also the history of revolutions. The seignorial rights which had been built up in France through centuries, and which were afterwards undermined by economic development during the course of centuries, were swept away by one blow on August 4,

1789. On November 9, 1918, the German revolution annihilated German absolutism, which had been undermined by the struggle of the proletariat and exploded by the victories of the Allies during the war. We have already mentioned that one of the war slogans of the British Government, of which Mr. Baldwin was a member, was " War until German militarism is completely smashed ! " Does not Mr. Baldwin think that in so far as the war catastrophe, in which Mr. Baldwin himself played a certain part, prepared a revolutionary catastrophe in Germany, all this took place with no little detriment to historical gradualness ? Of course, it may be objected that here the fault lies with German militarism and with the bad will of the Kaiser to boot. We will gladly believe that if Mr. Baldwin had created the world he would have peopled it with the most well-disposed of Kaisers and the most kind-hearted of militarists. But such an opportunity was not afforded the British Premier ; and indeed we have heard from him himself that people, including Kaisers, are born neither equal, nor good, nor fraternal. We must take the world as it is. More than that : if the break-up of German imperialism is a blessing, it has to be acknowledged that the German revolution, which consummated the work of war disintegration, was also a blessing ; in other words, a catastrophe which suddenly overthrew that which had been built up gradually was a blessing.

Mr. Baldwin may object, it is true, that all this has no direct relation to Britain, and that only in that chosen country has the principle of gradualness found its lawful expression. But if the matter stood thus, then Mr. Baldwin appealed in vain to my words, which had relation to Russia, giving by doing so a universal, general, absolute character to the principle of gradualness. My political experience does not confirm this. Within the term of my memory three revolutions have taken place in Russia: in 1905, in March 1917, and in November 1917. So far as the March revolution is concerned, a certain discreet co-operation with it was afforded by a gentleman not unknown to Mr. Baldwin —Buchanan—who evidently reckoned that a little revolutionary catastrophe in Petersburg would be more serviceable to Great Britain than the Rasputin kind of gradualness.

But is it true in the last resort that "the character and history of the British nation" is permeated to such a decided and absolute extent with the Conservative traditions of gradualness? Is it true that the British people are so hostile to "violent changes"? The whole history of Great Britain is first of all the history of revolutionary changes, which the British governing classes effected in the life . . . of other nations. Thus, for example, it would be interesting to know whether the seizure of Egypt or India may be interpreted in terms of the principle of gradualness? The policy of the British governing classes in relation to India is expressed most openly in the words of Lord Salisbury: "India must be bled!" It is not out of place to recall that Salisbury was the leader of the same party that is directed by Mr. Baldwin to-day. To this must be parenthetically added, that as the result of the excellently organised conspiracy of the bourgeois Press the British people actually do not know what is happening in India. (N.B.—And that is called democracy.) Perhaps we may recall the history of unfortunate Ireland, which is especially rich in manifestations of the peaceful evolutionary methods of action of the British governing classes? So far as we remember, the subjection of South Africa did not meet with the protests of Mr. Baldwin, and yet when the soldiers of General Roberts broke the defensive front of the Boer colonists, surely the latter did not see in that a specially convincing demonstration of gradualness! It is true that all this has reference to the *external* history of Britain. But none the less it is strange that the principle of evolutionary gradualness, which commends itself to us in the quality of a universal first cause, suspends its action beyond the confines of Great Britain—at the frontiers of China, when it is necessary to compel her by means of war to purchase opium; at the frontiers of Turkey, when it is necessary to take Mosul from her; at the frontiers of Persia and Afghanistan, when it is necessary to imbue them with humility before Britain. Is it not possible to draw from this the conclusion that the greater the success with which Britain applied force to other peoples, the greater was the degree of gradualness which she was able to realise within her own borders? Exactly so! During the course of three centuries Great Britain carried on an unbroken sequence of wars, so directed as by means of piracy and violence against other nations to enlarge the sphere of her exploitation, seize foreign wealth, kill foreign commercial competitors, annihilate foreign sea-power, and thus enrich the British ruling classes. A serious investigation of the facts and their internal associations inevitably leads to the conclusion that the governing classes of Britain were the better able to avoid revolutionary disturbances within their own country the more successful they were in increasing their own material power, by means of war and all kinds of general disturbances in other countries; thus, by means of timely concessions, always very niggardly, they maintained the possibility of staying the revolutionary agitation of the masses. But such a conclusion, irrefutable in itself, proves exactly the contrary of that which Mr. Baldwin desired to prove, since in actuality the very history of Great Britain testifies that "peaceful development" can only be ensured with the aid of a sequence of wars, colonial violences, and bloody disturbances. This has no resemblance to "gradualness"!

A well-known populariser of British history for the British masses, H. de B. Gibbins, writes in *The English People in the Nineteenth Century*: "English influence in foreign politics has *generally*, since 1815, been exercised in the direction of supporting movements for greater freedom and constitutional reform." This phrase is truly noteworthy: being profoundly official, "national," traditional, it does not leave the hypocritical doctrine of non-interference in the affairs of other nations a leg to stand on; at the same time it witnesses to the fact that Britain supported constitutional movements in other countries only in so far as such support was of service to her commercial and other interests; in the other case, as the inimitable Gibbins implies, there are exceptions to this rule. For the purpose of instructing her own people, all the past history of Great Britain, despite the doctrine of non-interference, is represented as having the quality of a glorious struggle of the British Government for freedom all over the earth. Thus every act of cunning and violence—the opium war with China, the enslaving of Egypt, the war with the Boers, intervention on behalf of Tsarist generals—all are explained as accidental exceptions to the rule. In that case, there are seen to be not a few holes in the doctrine of "gradualness" generally, both on the side of freedom and on the side of despotism.

One may of course go farther and say that in international relations violence is allowable and even inevitable, but between classes it is reprehensible. But then there is no point in talking about the natural law of gradualness, which is supposed to govern all development in nature and society. Then we must say straightforwardly that the oppressed class is bound to support the oppressor class of its own nation, when the latter applies force for its own ends ; but the oppressed class has no right to resort to force in order to ensure itself a better position in a society based on oppression. This will be not the " law of nature," but the law of the bourgeois criminal code.

However, even within the limits of the internal history of Great Britain the principle of gradual and peaceful development has not been by any means so governing a feature as the Conservative philosophers pretend. In the final reckoning all the contemporary history of Britain developed from the revolution of the seventeenth century. It is from the mighty civil war of that epoch that Tories and Whigs, who have alternately put their seal on British history during nearly three centuries, had their beginning. When Mr. Baldwin appeals to the Conservative traditions of British history, we allow ourselves to remind him that the tradition of the Conservative Party itself has its basis in the revolution of the middle of the seventeenth century. In equal measure the appeal to the " character of the English people " compels us to recall that this character was welded by the hammer of the civil war between Cavaliers and Roundheads. The character of the Independents ; of the petty bourgeoisie, traders, artisans, free landowners, the small local landlord nobility—of the practical, the religious, the economical, the industrious, the enterprising class—clashed inimically with the character of the slothful, dissolute, and arrogant governing classes of old England—the court nobility, titled bureacracy, and episcopacy. And yet both these and those were British! Oliver Cromwell, that heavy military hammer on the anvil of civil war, fashioned that same national character, which during the course of two centuries and a half ensured the gigantic advantages of the British bourgeoisie in the world struggle, in order afterwards, at the passing of the nineteenth century, to reveal itself as too conservative even from the point of view of capitalist development. It goes without saying that the struggle of the Long Parliament with the autocratic Government of Charles I and the austere dictatorship of Cromwell was led up to by the previous history of Britain. But that only means that revolutions are not made at pleasure, but break out organically from the conditions of social development, and are, though less obviously, just as inevitable a stage in the development of relationships between classes within the one nation as war is in the development of relationships between organised nations. Perhaps Mr. Baldwin will discover a fount of theoretical consolation in this gradualness of preparation.

Conservative old ladies, including Mrs. Snowden, who have recently discovered that the royal families constitute the most industrious class in society, must without doubt lie awake and shudder at nights when they recall the execution of Charles I. And meantime even the thoroughly reactionary Macaulay has come near to understanding this event. "Those who had him in their grip," he says, "were not midnight stabbers. What they did they did in order that it might be a spectacle to heaven and earth and that it might be held in everlasting remembrance.

They enjoyed keenly the very scandal which they gave. That the ancient constitution and the public opinion of England were directly opposed to regicide made regicide seem strangely fascinating to a party bent on effecting a complete political and social revolution. In order to accomplish their purpose, it was necessary that they should first break in pieces every part of the machinery of government; and this necessity was rather agreeable than painful to them. . . . A revolutionary tribunal was created. That tribunal pronounced Charles a tyrant, a traitor, a murderer, and a public enemy; and his head was severed from his shoulders before thousands of spectators in front of the banqueting-hall of his own palace." [1] From the point of view of the endeavours of the Puritans to break in pieces all sections of the old government machine, the circumstance that Charles Stuart was an extravagant, lying, and cowardly vagabond was quite a secondary consideration. The Puritans struck a mortal blow not only at Charles I but at royal absolutism—a blow the fruits of which the adherents of parliamentary gradualness enjoy to the present day.

The rôle of revolution in the general political and social development of Britain was not ended, however, with the seventeenth century. One may say—although it will sound paradoxical—that *all the later developments in Great Britain took place with the aid of European revolutions.* We shall here give only an outline of the most important incidents, which may perhaps be of value to others besides Mr. Baldwin.

The great French revolution gave a large impetus to the development of democratic tendencies in Great Britain, and, above all, to the workers' movement, which was driven underground by the exceptional laws

[1] Macaulay, *History of England*, chap. i.

of 1799. The war against revolutionary France was popular only among the governing classes ; the masses of the people sympathised with the French revolution, and demonstrated their anger with the Pitt Government. The formation of British trade unions was in large measure inspired by the influence of the French revolution on the British working masses.

The triumph of reaction on the continent, by increasing the importance of the landlords, led in 1814 to the restoration of the Bourbons in France and the introduction of the Corn Laws in Great Britain.

The July revolution of 1830 in France gave impetus to the first electoral Reform Bill in 1831 in Britain. The bourgeois revolution on the continent led to a bourgeois reform in the British Isles.

The radical reorganisation of the administration of Canada in the direction of a broad autonomy was carried out after the insurrection in Canada in 1837–38.

The revolutionary Chartist movement led in 1844–47 to the institution of the ten-hour working day, and in 1846 to the repeal of the Corn Laws. The break-up of the revolutionary movement in 1848 on the continent not only involved the decline of the Chartist movement, but also for long held up the democratisation of the British Parliament.

The electoral reform of 1868 was preceded by the civil war in the United States. When in 1861 the struggle broke out between North and South in America, the British workers demonstrated their sympathy with the Northern States, while the sympathy of the ruling classes was largely given to the slave-owners. It is instructive to note that the Liberal Palmerston, called the North "incendiary," and many of his colleagues, among whom was the illustrious Gladstone, sympathised with the South and were successful in gaining the recognition of the Southern States as not insurgents but a war party. Warships for the Southerners were built in British yards. None the less, the North was victorious, and this revolutionary victory on the territory of America *procured electoral rights to a section of the British working class* (the law of 1876). It is to the point to mention that in Great Britain itself the electoral reform was accompanied by a turbulent movement, which led to the " July days " of 1868, when great disorders lasted for two days.

The defeat of the revolution in 1848 weakened the British workers; the Russian revolution of 1905 immediately strengthened them. As the result of the General Election of 1906 the Labour Party for the first time formed a large fraction with forty-two members. Without doubt the influence of the 1905 revolution is manifest in this.

In 1918, before the end of the war, a new electoral reform was introduced in Great Britain, which greatly enlarged the ranks of worker voters, and for the first time permitted women to participate in the elections. Surely Mr. Baldwin will not trouble to deny that the Russian Revolution was an important motive for this reform. The British bourgeoisie reckoned that by such means a revolution could be avoided. It follows, therefore, that even for the introduction of reforms the principle of gradualness alone is insufficient, and that an actual threat of revolution is necessary.

If we thus review the history of Great Britain during the last century and a half against its background of general European and general world development, it appears that Britain exploited other countries not only economically but also politically, reducing its own "charges" at the expense of the civil wars of the peoples of Europe and America.

What was the thought behind the two phrases that Mr. Baldwin extracted from my book, in order to contrast them with the policy of the revolutionary representatives of the British proletariat? It will not be difficult to show that the direct and definite idea behind my words is entirely contrary to that which is necessary to Mr. Baldwin. The easier it was for the Russian proletariat to seize power, the greater were the obstacles it met with in its socialistic reconstruction. Yes, I said that and I repeat it. Our old ruling classes were economically and politically insignificant. Our parliamentary and democratic traditions were almost non-existent. It was easier for us to tear away the masses from the influence of the bourgeoisie and to overthrow their domination. But just because our bourgeoisie developed later and accomplished little, we received a scanty inheritance. We now have to lay down roads, build bridges and schools, teach the adults their letters, and so on; in other words, we have to execute the vast mass of economic and cultural work which the bourgeois regime has executed in the older capitalist countries. It was in this sense that I said, the easier it was for us to deal with the bourgeoisie, the more difficult it was for us in the matter of socialist reconstruction. But this direct political theorem connotes its converse: the richer and more cultured the country, the older her parliamentary democratic traditions, the more difficult it will be for the Communist Party to seize power; *but the swifter and more successfully will the work of socialist construction be carried through after the seizure of power.* Still more concretely: the overthrow of the domination of the British bourgeoisie is not an easy task; it demands an indispensable " gradualness," in other words, serious preparation ; but then, having seized power, the land, the industrial, commercial, and banking apparatus, the British proletariat will be able to carry out the reorganisation of the capitalist into a socialist economy with much fewer sacrifices, with much greater success, and at a much quicker tempo. That is the converse of the theorem, which I have more than once had to enunciate and to take as a general basis, and which has a direct relation to the question that interests Mr. Baldwin.

But that is not all. When I spoke of the difficulty of socialist reconstruction, I had in mind not only the backwardness of our country, but the gigantic opposition we had to face from outside. Mr. Baldwin knows doubtless that British Governments, of which he was a member, spent about a hundred million pounds sterling on military interventions and on the blockade of Soviet Russia. It is to the point to recall that the aim of these expensive enterprises was the overthrow of the Soviet Government. The British Conservatives and the British Liberals also—at any rate at that period—decisively rejected the principle of " gradualness " in reference to the Workers' and Peasants' Republic, and endeavoured to settle an historical question by means of a catastrophe. On the whole, it is sufficient to take up this one question in order to show that the whole philosophy of " gradualness " is extraordinarily similar to the morality of those monks who themselves drank wine and recommended water to their flock.[1]

[1] We have no desire to be indiscreet, and so will not ask in what measure false documents, for instance, attributed to foreign States and made use of for election purposes may be regarded as an instrument of " gradualness " in the development of so-called Christian morality in a civilised society ? But while we refrain from asking this ticklish question, we cannot forbear to recall that even on the testimony of Napoleon the falsification of diplomatic documents was never resorted to so extensively as in British diplomacy. And since that time technique has made huge strides forward.

Whether that be so or not, the Russian workers, having seized power, found first of all Germany against them, and then all the countries of the Entente, directed by Britain and France. The British proletariat, when it seizes power, will not have against itself either the Russian Tsar or the Russian bourgeoisie. On the contrary, it will be able to depend on the gigantic material and human resources of our Soviet Union, for—and we do not conceal this from Mr. Baldwin—the affairs of the British proletariat will be at least in as much measure our affairs as the affairs of the Russian bourgeoisie were, and essentially remain, the affairs of the British Conservatives.

It is not questioned that, as Mr. Baldwin points out, we are striving for the greater productivity of labour. Without that it would be useless to think about the raising of the well-being and culture of the Russian people, and that is the basic purpose of Communism. But the Russian worker is working to-day for himself. Having taken into their own hands an economic system, ruined first by the imperialist war, then by the civil war, nourished on interventions and blockade, the workers of Russia have now succeeded in raising their industry, which was almost defunct in 1921, to an average of 60 per cent. of its pre-war productivity. This achievement, although it is small in comparison with our aims, represents an indubitable and important success. If the one hundred million pounds sterling which Britain spent on attempts at a catastrophic revolution had been put into the Soviet economic system in the form of a loan or concession capital for its *gradual* uplift, we should by now without doubt have passed the pre-war level, paid British capital high rates of interest, and, what is most important, should have presented a large and continually growing market for her. It is not our fault if Mr. Baldwin violated the principle of gradualness just at that very point where it was not necessary to do so. But even with our present very low standard of industry, the position of the workers has greatly improved by comparison with recent years. When we reach the pre-war level—and that is a matter of the next two or three years—the position of our workers will be immeasurably better than it was before the war. Just because of that, and only because of that, we consider ourselves justified in calling the Russian proletariat to an increase in the productivity of their labour. It is one thing to work in workshops, factories, yards, and mines belonging to capitalists, and another to work on their own property. There is a great difference in that, Mr. Baldwin! And when the British workers control the mighty means of production which they and their predecessors have created, they will endeavour with all their powers to raise the level of production. This is very necessary to British industry, for despite its great achievements, it is completely enmeshed in the entanglements of its own past. Baldwin seems to know this; at any rate, in that same speech he said: "We owe our position and our place in the world largely to the fact that we were the first nation to endure the pangs which brought the industrial age into the world, but we are also paying the price of that privileged priority, and the price in part is our badly planned and congested towns, our back-to-back houses, our ugly factories, and our smoke-laden atmosphere." To this must be added the disintegrated character of British industry, its technical conservatism, its inadequate organisational flexibility. It is because of these things that British industry calls "pass" to-day to German and American industry. In order to save itself British industry needs an extensive and bold reorganisation. It is necessary to contemplate the foundations and the sub-foundations of Britain as the bases of a single economic system. Only thus can the coal industry be reorganised on healthy bases. The electrical economy of Britain is distinguished for its disintegratedness and backwardness ; attempts to nationalise it come up against the opposition of private interests at every step. Not only are the British towns, owing to their historical origins, stupidly planned ; all British industry, " gradually " accumulating, is void of system and plan. A new life can be poured into it only if it is approached as a single whole. But that is inconceivable while private ownership in the means of production is retained. The chief end of Socialism is the raising of the economic might of the people. Only on that basis is the construction of a more cultured, more harmonious, more happy human society conceivable. If Mr. Baldwin, with all his sympathies for ancient British industry, is compelled to confess that the new capitalistic forms—trusts and syndicates—represent a step forward, then we consider that a single socialistic combine of industry represents a gigantic step forward by comparison with capitalist trusts. But that programme cannot be realised without the transfer of all the means of production to the hands of the working class, not, in other words, without the expropriation of the bourgeoisie. Baldwin himself reminds us of the " titanic forces let loose by the industrial revolution of the eighteenth century, which changed the face of the country and all the features of our national life." Why in this case does Mr. Baldwin talk of revolution, and not of gradual development ? Because at the end of the eighteenth century a radical change took place in a short period, which led in particular to the expropriation of the petty industrialists. It ought to be clear to all who have regard to the essential logic of an historical process, that the industrial revolution of the eighteenth century, which regenerated Great Britain from top to bottom, would have been impossible without the political revolution of the seventeenth century. Without a revolution made in the name of bourgeois might and bourgeois abilities, against aristocratic privileges and courtly indolence, the great spirit of technical inventions would not have been aroused, and there would have been no one to apply them to industrial purposes. The political revolution of the seventeenth century, which grew out of all the foregoing development, prepared the way for the industrial revolution of the eighteenth century. Britain, like all capitalist countries, now needs an economic revolution far excelling in its historical significance the industrial revolution of the eighteenth century. But this new economic revolution—the reconstruction of the whole economic system on one socialist plan—cannot be settled without a preliminary political revolution. Private ownership in the means of production is now a much greater obstacle on the road of economic development than were in their time the craft privileges which were the form of petty-bourgeois ownership. As the bourgeoisie will not under any circumstances renounce their ownership rights of their own free will, a bold revolutionary force must inevitably be put in motion. Until now history has not thought out any other method. And there will not be any exception in the case of Britain.

As for the second quotation ascribed to me by Mr. Baldwin, I here am greatly perplexed. I categorically deny that I anywhere and at any time could say seemingly that there is an unchangeable nature of the

Russian against which the revolution was impotent. Where is this quotation from? From long experience I know that not all people, not even Prime Ministers, quote exactly. Quite by accident I came across a passage in my pamphlet *Problems of Cultural Work* which has a full and complete reference to the question interesting us. I quote this passage in its entirety:—

"What are the foundations for our hopes of victory? The first is that a critical faculty and an activity has been aroused in our people masses. Through revolution our people have opened for themselves a window to Europe—understanding by 'Europe,' culture—as two hundred years or more previously the Russia of Peter opened not a window, but a casement into Europe for the upper groups of the nobility and bureaucratic state authorities. These passive qualities of meekness and humility, which according to the officially or voluntarily simple ideologues were declared to be the specific, unchangeable, and sacred qualities of the Russian people, and which were in actuality only the expression of its slavish subjection and cultural backwardness—these miserable, shameful qualities received their death-blow in October 1917. That does not mean, of course, that we now do not bear in ourselves the inheritance of the past. We do and shall for long bear it. But a great break with the past, not only material but spiritual, has been achieved. No one now dares to recommend the Russian people to build their destiny on the foundation of meekness, humility, and long-suffering. No, from henceforth the virtues entering more and more deeply into the consciousness of the people are: a critical faculty, activity, and collective creation. And on this greatest conquest of the national character is founded more than on anything else our hope in the success of all our labour."

As we see, this has very little resemblance to that which Mr. Baldwin ascribes to me. In his justification it has to be said that the British constitution does not lay on the Premier the obligation of quoting accurately. As for precedents, which play such a great part in the life of Britain, there is no lack of them in any case: what is the value of one William Pitt in the realm of false citations?

It may be objected: Is there any sense in arguing about revolution with the leader of the Tories? What significance can the historical philosophy of the Conservative Premier have for the working class? But here the nail is hit on the head: the philosophy of MacDonald, Snowden, Webb, and other leaders of the Labour Party, is only the echo of the historical theories of Baldwin. A little later we shall demonstrate that, with all the necessary . . . gradualness.

III

CERTAIN "PECULIARITIES" OF BRITISH LABOUR LEADERS

AFTER the death of Curzon the leaders of the parties and others delivered speeches of eulogy. In the House of Commons the Socialist MacDonald ended with these words: "He was a great public servant, a man who was a fine colleague, a man who had a very noble ideal of public duty, which may well be emulated by his successors." That about Curzon! When workers protested against this speech, the *Daily Herald*, the organ of the Labour Party, printed the protests under the unpretentious heading: "Another Point of View." A sage editorship thus evidently desired to say that besides the court, Byzantine, sycophantic, crawling point of view there was also that of the workers.

At the beginning of April the not altogether unknown Labour leader, Thomas, Secretary of the National Union of Railwaymen, and former Secretary for the Colonies, participated with the Prime Minister Baldwin in a banquet given by the administration of the Great Western Railway Company. At one time Baldwin was a director of this company, and Thomas worked under him as a stoker. With magnificent patronage Mr. Baldwin spoke of his "friend" Jimmy Thomas, and Thomas proposed a toast to the directors of the "Great Western" and to its chairman, Lord Churchill.

Thomas spoke with deep feeling of Mr. Baldwin, who—only think of it!—all his life had followed in the footsteps of his venerable father. They would attack him (Thomas)—said this absolutely unprecedented lackey—on account of the banquet and for his intercourse with Baldwin as a traitor to his own class, but he (Thomas) did not belong to any class, since truth was not the property of any class.

On the occasion of the debates instituted on the initiative of the " left-wing " Labour M.P.s on the assignation of money to the Prince of Wales for his travels abroad, the same *Daily Herald* burst out with a leading article on relations to the royal authority. Anybody who concluded from the debates that the Labour Party desired to destroy the royal authority, wrote the paper, would commit an error. But, on the other hand, it was impossible not to note that the Royal Family were not improving their position in the general opinion of intelligent people: there was too much pomp and ceremony, suggested it may be by " unintelligent counsellors "; too much attention to horse-races with the inevitable totalisator; in addition the Duke and Duchess of York when in East Africa hunted rhinoceroses and other animals deserving of a better fate. Of course—the paper reflects—to lay the blame entirely on the Royal Family is impossible; tradition binds them too closely to the existence and habits of one class. But it is necessary to make efforts to break with these traditions. That is, in our opinion, not only desirable, but absolutely indispensable. An occupation should be found for the heir to the throne which would transform him into a part of the government machine, and so on, and so forth, in the same habitually insipid, habitually stupid, habitually lackey-like tone. So in our own country in the past, for example in 1905 or 1906, might the organ of the Samaran peaceful regenerators have written.

The ubiquitous Mrs. Snowden got entangled with the Royal Family affair, and in a short letter she stated that only the throaty orators of the street corners could not know and understand that the Royal Families belonged to the most hardworking elements of Europe. And as the Bible itself says: "Thou shalt not muzzle the ox when he treadeth out the corn," it goes without saying that Mrs. Snowden is in favour of voting money for the travels of the Prince of Wales.

"I am a Socialist, democrat, and Christian," this person once wrote, in explaining why she was against Bolshevism. That, however, is not a complete catalogue of Mrs. Snowden's qualities. Out of politeness we shall not name the others.

The worthy Dr. Shiels, Labour M.P. for East Edinburgh, explained in a newspaper that the travels of the Prince of Wales were good for trade, and consequently for the working class. Therefore he was in favour of voting the money.

Let us now take someone from the "left" or semi-left Labour M.P.s. The question of certain ownership rights of the Scottish Church was being discussed in Parliament. The Scottish Labour M.P., Johnston, taking as basis the "Act of Security" of 1707, denied the right of the British Parliament to interfere with the solemnly recognised rights of the Scottish Church. The Speaker refused to remove the question from the order of the day. At that a second Scottish M.P., Maclean, declared that if the Bill were passed he and his friends would return to Scotland and would call for the Treaty of Union between England and Scotland to be recognised as annulled and for a Scottish Parliament to be set up. (Laughter from the Conservatives and assent from the Scottish members of the Labour Party.) Here everything is instructive. The Scottish group, standing on the left wing of the Labour group in Parliament, protests against clerical legislation, not on the principle of the separation of Church from State, or other considerations of real value, but taking as basis the sacred rights of the Scottish Church, secured to her by a treaty already more than two centuries old. In revenge for the violation of the rights of the Scottish Church these same Labour M.P.s threaten to demand the re-establishment of the Scottish Parliament, for which in itself they have absolutely no need.

George Lansbury, a left Pacifist, in a leading article in the daily organ of the Labour Party, tells how at a meeting in Monmouthshire the men and women workers sang a religious hymn with the greatest of enthusiasm, and how that hymn " helped " him (Lansbury). Individuals may deny religion, he says, but the Labour Movement, as a movement, cannot reconcile itself to that. Our struggle has need of enthusiasm, of devotion and fidelity, and it is impossible to achieve this by appealing only to personal interests. In that case, if our movement has need of enthusiasm, it is itself without power to evoke it, according to Lansbury, and is compelled to borrow it from the clergy.

John Wheatley, former Minister for Health in MacDonald's Cabinet, is regarded as almost extreme left. None the less, Wheatley is not only a Socialist but also a Catholic. To put it more correctly : he is first of all a Catholic, and only afterwards a Socialist. As the Pope of Rome has called for a struggle with Communism and Socialism, the editorship of the *Daily Herald*, out of politeness forbearing to mention the Holy Father, approached Wheatley with a request to explain how the matter stood with regard to the mutual relations between Catholicism and Socialism. It is needless to suppose that the paper asked whether a Socialist can be a Catholic, or for that matter a believer of any kind; no, the question was asked whether a Catholic was allowed to be a Socialist. The obligation of a human being to be a believer is beyond all doubt: the only matter in question is the right of a believer to be a Socialist and remain a good Catholic. In his answer, the "left-wing" Wheatley took the same attitude. He considered that Catholicism takes no part directly in politics, but defines "only" the moral laws of conduct and binds the Socialist to apply his political principles with the "necessary attention to the moral rights of others." Wheatley suggests that the policy of the British party in this question is the only right one, since, in distinction from continental Socialism, it has not taken on an "anti-Christian" direction. For this "left-winger" Socialist policy is directed by personal morality, and personal morality by religion. In no respect does this differ from the philosophy of Lloyd George, who regards the Church as the central electric station for all parties. Compromise here receives its religious sanctification.

Concerning the M.P. Kirkwood, who made an attack on the travelling money of the Prince of Wales, one of the Socialists wrote in the *Daily Herald* that he (Kirkwood) had in his veins a drop of the blood of old Cromwell, evidently using the words in the sense of revolutionary determination. Whether that is so we as yet do not know. In any event, Kirkwood inherited piety from Cromwell. In his parliamentary speech Kirkwood explained that he had no kind of personal account to settle with the Prince, and had no envy of him. "The Prince has nothing to give me. I enjoy excellent health. I have possession of my independence as a human being, and there is only one before whom I am responsible for my actions—that is my Maker." Thus we learn from this speech not only that a certain Scottish M.P. enjoys excellent health, but also that he explains his very origins not by the laws of biology and physiology, but by the design of a certain Creator, with whom Mr. Kirkwood maintains a thoroughly definite relationship, based on the one hand on personal favour, and on the other on a grateful obligation.

One could enlarge at will the number of such examples many times. To put it more correctly, almost all the political activity of the upper groups of the Labour Party could be analysed into that kind of episode, which at first glance seems a laughable or unseemly curiosity, but in which in actuality is reproduced the peculiarities of all past history, just as, for example, the complicated processes of an organism are reproduced in bladder stones. Here we desire it to be borne in mind that the "organic" character of the origins of these or other peculiarities does not in the least exclude the possibility of surgical intervention with a view to their removal.

The doctrine of the leaders of the Labour Party is a kind of amalgam of Conservatism and Liberalism, partially adapted to the needs of trade unions, or rather to their upper groups. They are all afflicted with the religion of "gradualness." Moreover, they confess the religion of the Old and the New Testament. They all consider themselves ultra-civilised people, and at the same time believe that the Heavenly Father created humanity in order afterwards out of the abundance of His love to curse it, and also in the sequel to attempt by the crucifixion of His own Son to amend somewhat this extremely tangled business. Such national institutions as the trade union bureaucracy, the first Ministry of MacDonald, and Mrs. Snowden, grew out of the spirit of Christianity.

With the religion of gradualness and the Calvinistic religion of predestination is closely linked the religion of national arrogance. MacDonald is convinced that since his bourgeoisie was formerly the premier bourgeoisie of the world, he has absolutely nothing to learn from the barbarians and semi-barbarians of the European continent. In this respect, as in all others, MacDonald only apes the bourgeois leaders, such as Canning, who declared—albeit with much greater foundation—that there was no point in parliamentary Britain learning its politics from the peoples of Europe. In monotonously appealing to the Conservative traditions of the political development of Britain, Baldwin appeals undoubtedly to the mighty support of the bourgeois dominance in the past. The bourgeoisie were able to imbue the upper circles of the Labour Party with Conservatism. It was not an accident that the most determined fighters for Chartism came from the artisan strata, proletarianised in the space of two generations by the pressure of capitalism. It is just as noteworthy that the most radical elements of the contemporary British Labour movement are mostly of Scotch or Irish race. (This law is not extended, of course, to cover the Scotsman MacDonald.) The union in Ireland of social with national oppression, in face of the sharp conflict of an agrarian with a capitalist country, gives the conditions for sharp changes in consciousness. Scotland set out upon the road of capitalism later than England; a sharper break in the life of the masses of the people causes a sharper break in political reaction. If the British "socialist" gentlemen were able to give some time to reflection on their own history, especially on the rôle of Ireland and Scotland, they might perhaps be able to understand why and in what fashion backward Russia, with her sharp transition to capitalism, thrust upward the most determinedly revolutionary party, and was the first to set out on the road of socialist change.

None the less, the stagnant conservatism of British existence is to-day undermined irredeemably. For decades the "leaders" of the British working class considered that an independent Labour Party was the mournful privilege of continental Europe. Not a trace is left to-day of that naïve and doltish self-conceit. The proletariat has forced the trade unions to create an independent party. But the matter will not rest there. The Liberal and semi-Liberal leaders of the Labour Party still think that the social revolution is the mournful privilege of the European continent. And their backwardness will be revealed by events. A great deal less time will be necessary to turn the Labour Party into a revolutionary party than was needed for its creation.

The most important element in the conservatism of political development was, and to a certain extent still remains, the religiosity of the British people with Protestantism as a basis. Puritanism was the school of a harsh experience, of a social training of the middle classes. The masses of the people, however, always opposed it. The proletariat do not think of themselves as "chosen." There is clearly no Calvinistic predestination in them. On the foundation of the Independents was built up British Liberalism, the chief mission of which was to educate, in other words to bring the working masses into subjection to bourgeois society. Within certain limits and down to a certain period

Liberalism fulfilled this mission, but in the final resort it was as little able to remould the working class as was Puritanism. To replace the Liberals came the Labour Party, with the same traditions—Puritan and Liberal. If we were to take the Labour Party only in its MacDonald, Henderson, and company section, we should have to declare that they came to consummate the uncompleted work of total enslavement of the working class to bourgeois society. But in actuality a second process is, despite them, at work in the masses, a process which must finally liquidate the Puritan-Liberal traditions, liquidating MacDonald in its development.

For the British middle classes, Catholicism, as also Anglicanism, was a tradition ready to hand, bound up with the privileges of the nobility and clergy. The young British bourgeoisie created Protestantism in contra-distinction to Catholicism and Anglicanism, as being their own form of faith and as the vindication of their own place in society.

Calvinism, with its iron predestination, was a mystic form of approach to the systematisation of an historical process. The rising bourgeoisie felt that the laws of history were on its side, and this its consciousness it clothed in the form of the doctrine of predestination. The Calvinistic denial of free will in no wise paralysed the revolutionary energy of the Independents; on the contrary, it provided a mighty rallying point for it. The Independents felt that they were called to fulfil a great historic act. One may with a certain justice draw an analogy between the doctrine of predestination in the Puritan revolution and the rôle of Marxism in the revolution of the proletariat. But in the one and in the other a tremendous activity is based not on a subjective arbitrariness, but on an iron systematisation—in the one case mystically and in the other scientifically known.

The British proletariat accepted Protestantism as a tradition ready to hand, that is, as the bourgeoisie down to the seventeenth century accepted Catholicism and Anglicanism. Just as the awakened bourgeoisie set up Protestantism against Catholicism, so the revolutionary proletariat will set up materialism and atheism against Protestantism.

If for Cromwell and his followers Calvinism was a spiritual weapon for the revolutionary transformation of society, to MacDonald it only suggests a reverent attitude to all that which has been " gradually " created. The MacDonalds inherited from Puritanism not its revolutionary strength, but its religious prejudices. From the Owenites they received not their communistic fervour, but their Utopian hostility to the class struggle. From the past political history of Britain the Fabians borrowed only the mental dependence of the proletariat on the bourgeoisie. History turned its nether parts to these gentlemen ; and the writings that they there read became their programme.

Island position, wealth, the success of their world policy—all this cemented together by Puritanism, by the religion of a " chosen people," was transformed into a haughty disdain generally for everything continental and non-British. The middle classes of Britain were long convinced that the languages, science, technique, and culture of other nations were not worth their study. All this was imitated in its entirety by the Philistines at the head of the Labour Party to-day.

It is curious that even Hyndman, who while Marx was still alive published a book *England for All*, took as his basis in that book the author of *Capital*, without naming either him or his work. The reason of this strange silence was that Hyndman had no desire to shock the Britishers; was it at all conceivable that a Britisher could learn anything from a German!

In this regard historical dialectic played an evil game with Britain, transforming the advantages of her earlier development into the causes of backwardness. We see this in the realm of industry, in science, in the state structure, and in political ideology. She was not able to search for and find in one of the leading countries an indication of her own future. She moved forward gropingly, empirically, drawing generalisations from her road and looking ahead only in so far as it was unavoidable. The traditional way of thought of the British, that is first of all of the British bourgeoisie, is impressed with the stamp of empiricism, and that mental tradition has passed over to the upper circles of the working class. Empiricism became a tradition and a standard, in other words, it united with a contemptuous attitude towards the "abstract" way of thought of the continent. Germany for long years philosophised over the elemental nature of the State, while the British bourgeoisie constructed a State most perfect of its kind for the convenience of their own domination. But with the passing of time it was seen that the German bourgeoisie, backward in practice, and therefore inclined to theoretical speculations, were much more scientifically organised and adapted to the struggle for the world market. The British socialist Philistines adopted from their bourgeoisie a haughty attitude to the continent at that moment when the former preponderance of Britain had been completely overthrown.

MacDonald, in justifying the "natural" peculiarities of British Socialism, states that in looking for its ideological origins we "must pass by Marx to Godwin."

Godwin was a great figure for his time. But for the British to return to him is the same as if the Germans were to seek origins in Weitling or the Russians in Chernishevsky. We have no desire to imply that there are no " peculiarities " in the British Labour Movement. It was the Marxian school that always devoted great attention to the oddity of the British development. But we find the explanation of this oddity in objective conditions, in the structure of society and its changes. Thanks to this, we, Marxians, understand the tempo of development of the British Labour Movement and foresee its morrow much better than do the present " theoreticians " of the Labour Party. The call of the ancient philosophy to " know thyself " has not rung in their ears. They consider that they are called by destiny to reconstruct anew the most ancient of social structures, and at the same time they are completely prostrated before any projection of the lines into the realm of actuality. How can they make an attack on bourgeois private ownership when they have not the courage to refuse pocket-money to the Prince of Wales ?

The royal authority, they declare, " does not hinder " the progress of the country, and works out cheaper than a president, if all the expenses of election, etc., are taken into consideration. Such speeches from the workers' leaders characterise that aspect of the " oddity " which it is impossible to call other than a conservative clownishness. The royal authority is weak, so long as the instrument of bourgeois domination is the bourgeois Parliament, and so long as the bourgeoisie has no need of extra-parliamentary methods of action. But in case of need the bourgeoisie can make use of the royal authority with great success, as the concentration point for all the extra-parliamentary, that is to say, the real forces directed against the working class. The

British bourgeoisie itself, when in a similar position, knew perfectly the danger of even the most fictitious monarchy. Thus, in 1837 the British Government abolished the title of Great Mogul in India, expelling its bearer from the sacred city of Delhi, despite the fact that that title had become a purely nominal one by that time. For the British bourgeoisie understood that given certain conditions the Great Mogul might focus the struggle of the Indian upper classes against the British sovereignty.

To proclaim a socialist programme and at the same time to declare that the royal authority "does not hinder" and works out cheaper, is absolutely the same as, for example, acknowledging materialistic science and making use of the incantation of a sorcerer for toothache, on the ground that the sorcerer is cheaper. In such a little "detail" the whole man is revealed, all the fiction of his acknowledgment of materialistic science and all the falseness of his system of ideas. For a socialist the question of the monarchy is not decided from the point of view of to-day's accountancy, still less when it is a false accountancy. It is a question of the complete transformation of society, of its cleansing from all elements of slavery. That work makes a reconciliation with the monarchy both politically and psychologically impossible.

Mr. MacDonald, Mr. Thomas, and others are disturbed by those workers who protested when their Ministry decked themselves out in the ridiculous Court dress. Of course, that is not the chief of MacDonald's crimes; but it excellently symbolises all the others. When the young bourgeoisie fought with the nobility, it rejected ringlets and silk coats. The bourgeois revolutionaries wore the black dress of the Puritans. In contradistinction to the Cavaliers, the name of Roundheads was given to them. A new content seeks for itself a new form. Of course, the form of dress is only a conventionality, but the masses have no wish to understand, and rightly, why the representatives of the working class must subject themselves to the ridiculous conventions of a monarchical masquerade. And the masses are more and more coming to understand that he who is unfaithful in few things will be unfaithful also in many things.

We see the traits of conservatism, religiosity, and national arrogance in different degrees and in different combinations in all the present-day official leaders, from ultra-right Thomas to the left-wing Kirkwood. It would be a great error to underestimate the powers of resistance and tenacity of these conservative peculiarities of the upper ranks of the British working class. By this, of course, we have no wish to imply that clerical and conservative-national tendencies are completely foreign to the masses. But at the same time, while the bourgeois-national traits have entered into the flesh and blood of the leaders and the pupils of the Liberal Party, in the working masses they have an immeasurably less profound and stable character. We have already mentioned that Puritanism, the religion of the wealth-getting classes, did not succeed in penetrating deeply into the consciousness of the working masses. The same applies to Liberalism. The workers voted for Liberals, but remained workers in the mass, and the Liberals had always to be on the alert. The very displacing of the Liberal Party by a Labour Party was the result of the pressure of the proletarian masses. Under other conditions—in other words, if Britain were to gain strength and develop economically—the present-day type of Labour Party might continue and extend the "educational" work of Protestantism and Liberalism, that is, it might bind the consciousness of large circles of the working class more tightly to the conservative-national traditions and discipline of the bourgeois order. But under the present conditions of the open economic decline of Britain and the absence of prospects, a development in the diametrically opposite direction is to be expected. The war had already given a severe blow to the traditional religiosity of the British masses. Not for nothing was Mr. H. G. Wells occupied with the creation of a new religion, endeavouring *en route* from earth to Mars to carve out for himself the career of a Fabian Calvin. We utterly doubt his possibility of success. The hive of revolution swarms too well this time! The working masses will turbulently liberate themselves from the national-conservative discipline, working out their own discipline of revolutionary activity. Faced with this pressure from below, the upper ranks of the Labour Party will quickly change their colour. We do not by that wish to imply that MacDonald will change colour into a revolutionary. But those who in all probability will form the first substitutes, people of the type of Wheatley, Lansbury, and Kirkwood, will inevitably reveal that they are only a left variety of the same fundamentally Fabian type. Such radicalism is limited by democracy and religion, and poisoned with the national arrogance, which mentally enslaves the British bourgeoisie. In all probability the working class will have to renew their directive formation several times before they create a party actually answering to the historical situation and tasks of the British proletariat.

IV

THE FABIAN "THEORY" OF SOCIALISM

WE will exert the will-power necessary and read through an article by Ramsay MacDonald, in which he gave an exposition of his opinions not long before his resignation of office.[1] We warn our readers beforehand that we have to enter the ideological shop of an old-furniture dealer, where the stifling scent of napthalene does not interfere with the successful work of the moths.

"In the realm of feeling and conscience," MacDonald begins, "in the realm of spirit, Socialism forms the religion of service to the people." In those words is immediately betrayed the benevolent bourgeois, the left Liberal, who "serves" the people, coming to them from one side, or more truly from above. Such an approach has its roots entirely in the dim past, when the radical intelligentsia went to live in the working-class districts of London in order to carry on cultural and educational work. What a monstrous anachronism these words seem in reference to the present Labour Party, directly based as it is on the trade unions!

The word "religion" is not here to be understood simply in a rhetorical sense. It is a question of Christianity in the Anglo-Saxon interpretation. "Socialism is founded on the Gospels," proclaims MacDonald.

[1] The English text is translated from the Russian, which in turn was translated from the Prague Social-Revolutionary journal, *People's Will*.

"It denotes a well thought out (if only it did!) and determined attempt to Christianise Government and society." But in our opinion certain difficulties are met with along this road. *First:* The peoples who are reckoned according to statistics as Christian form approximately 37 per cent. of humanity. What is to happen to the non-Christian world? *Second:* Atheism is having not a small success among Christian peoples, and among the proletariat especially at that. This is less noticeable so far in the Anglo-Saxon countries. But humanity, even the Christian part of it, is not composed entirely of Anglo-Saxons. In the Soviet Union, numbering 130 million souls, atheism is the officially proclaimed State doctrine. *Third:* The domination of India by Great Britain has lasted now for hundreds of years. The European nations, with this same Britain at their head, long ago made a road to China. None the less, the number of atheists in Europe grows more quickly than the number of Christians in India and China. Why? Because Christianity appears before the Chinese and Indians as the religion of oppressors, violators, slave-owners, mighty despoliators, feloniously bursting into another's house. The Chinese know that Christian missionaries are sent in order to prepare the way for cruisers. There is the real, historical, actual Christianity! And this Christianity is the basis of Socialism? For China and India? *Fourth:* Christianity, according to official estimates, has existed 1,925 years. Before it became the religion of MacDonald it was the religion of the Roman thralls, of the nomad barbarians who settled in Europe, the religion of crowned and uncrowned despots and feudalists, the religion of the Inquisition, the religion of Charles Stuart, and under another guise the religion of Cromwell, who cut off

Charles Stuart's head. Finally, at the moment it is the religion of Lloyd George, Churchill, *The Times*, and, we must suppose, of that devout Christian who forged the "Zinoviev" letter to the glory of the Conservative election of the most Christian of democracies. In what fashion did Christianity, which through two thousand years, by the aid of sermons, scholastic violence, intimidations with suffering beyond the grave, hell fire, and the sword of the police, took root in the consciousness of the European nations and was transformed into their official religion—in what fashion did it lead in the twentieth century of its existence to the most bloody and evil of wars, after the previous nineteen centuries of Christian history had also been centuries of brutality and crime? And where in reality are there reasonable bases for hope that the "divine teaching" must in the twentieth, twenty-first, or twenty-fifth century of its history raise up equality and fraternity where it consecrated violence and subjection? It would be useless to expect from MacDonald an answer of a scholastic nature to these questions. Our wiseacre is an evolutionist, that is to say, he believes that everything "gradually" changes, and with divine assistance, for the better. MacDonald is an evolutionist, he does not believe in miracles, except that one unique miracle which took place 1,925 years ago: when into organic evolution butted in none other than the Son of God, putting into circulation a certain number of heavenly elements, from which the clergy gather an abundant earthly revenue.

The Christian basis of Socialism is enunciated in two decisive phrases of his article. "Who can deny that poverty is an evil, not only personal, but social? *Who does not feel compassion for poverty?*" Here behind the theory of Socialism is betrayed the philosophy of a socially minded philanthropic bourgeois, who feels "compassion" for the poor, and out of that compassion makes a "religion of his own conscience," not overmuch violating his business habits, for that matter.

Who does not feel compassion for poverty? All the history of Britain, as is well known, is the history of the compassion of her possessing classes for the poverty of the working class. Without going far back into the centuries, it is sufficient to investigate that history only, shall we say, from the sixteenth century, from the period of the enclosures of the peasants' land; in other words, the transformation of the majority of the peasants into homeless vagabonds, when compassion for poverty found its expression in the prisons, gallows, lopping of ears, and other measures of Christian commiseration. The Countess of Sutherland finished with her enclosures in the north of Scotland at the beginning of last century, and the moving story of this hangman business was told by Marx in immortal lines, in which, of course, we do not meet with a slobbering commiseration, but find instead a passionate revolutionary indignation.

Who does not feel compassion for poverty? Read through the history of Britain's industrial development, and in particular the exploitation of child labour. The compassion of the rich for poverty has never safeguarded the poor from degradation and misery. In Britain no less than anywhere else poverty has gained something for itself only in those cases where it succeeded in taking wealth by the throat. Surely it is not necessary to prove that, in a country with an age-old history of class struggle, which was also the history of churlish concessions and ruthless punishment?

"Socialism does not believe in force," MacDonald continues. "Socialism is a mental healthiness, and not a mental sickness. . . . And therefore by its very nature it must repudiate force with horror. It fights only with mental and moral weapons." All this is excellent, although it is not altogether new; in the Sermon on the Mount these same thoughts were expounded, although in a much better style. We have already recalled above whither all this leads. It is not clear to us why the untalented MacDonald paraphrase of the Sermon on the Mount should give better results. Tolstoy, who had at his command much mightier means of ideological conviction, did not succeed in attracting even the members of his own landlord family to the evangelical covenants. MacDonald was instructive on the question of the impermissibility of force when he was at the head of the Government. We remind our readers that during that time the police were not disbanded, the courts were not abolished, the prisons were not pulled down, the warships were not sunk—on the contrary, they built new ones. But so far as we can judge, the police, courts, prisons, the army and the fleet are all organs of force. The recognition of the truth that "Socialism is a mental healthiness and not a mental sickness" does not in the least hinder MacDonald from marching in the sacred footsteps of the great Christian Curzon in India and Egypt. In the quality of Christian, MacDonald recoils from violence with "horror"; in his capacity as Premier he applies all the methods of capitalist repression, and hands over the instruments of force to his Conservative successor inviolate. What in the last resort does the repudiation of force signify in practice? Only this, that the oppressed must not apply force against a capitalist

State ; nor the workers against the bourgeoisie, farmers against landlords, the Indians against the British administration and British capital. The State—created with the instrumentality of force by the monarchy against the people, by the bourgeoisie against the workers, by the landlords against the farmers, by officers against soldiers, by the Anglo-Saxon slave-owners against the colonial peoples, by " Christians " against pagans—this blood-imbued apparatus of a century-old force inspires MacDonald merely to a reverent obeisance. He feels horror only in regard to liberating force. In this consists the sacred essence of his " religion of service to the people."

" There is an old and a new school of Socialism," MacDonald says. " We belong to the new school." MacDonald's " ideal " (he has an " ideal ") is the same as that of the old school, but in addition the new school has a " better plan " for the realisation of this ideal. In what does this plan consist ? MacDonald does not leave us without an answer. " We have no class-consciousness. Our opponents are the people with class-consciousness. . . . But in place of a class-consciousness we desire to evoke the consciousness of social solidarity." Pouring out still more from the empty to the emptier, MacDonald concludes : " The class struggle is not made by us. It is created by capitalism, and will always be its fruit, just as thistles will always be the fruits of thistles." That MacDonald is without class-consciousness and that the leaders of the bourgeoisie have such a consciousness is quite indisputable, and signifies in essence that the British Labour Party goes at present without a head on its shoulders, while the British bourgeois parties have such a head, and one with a very powerful brow and a not

less powerful napc at that. And if MacDonald confined himself to the confession that he is a little weak in the head so far as "consciousness" is concerned, we should have no grounds for dispute. But MacDonald desires to formulate a programme out of his head with its weak consciousness. Under no circumstances can we agree to that.

"The class struggle," says MacDonald, "is created by capitalism." That of course is incorrect. The class struggle existed before capitalism. But it is true that the *contemporary* class struggle, that between the proletariat and the bourgeoisie, was created by capitalism. It is also true that it will "always be its fruit," in other words, it will exist so long as capitalism exists. But there are evidently two parties to a war. One of them is composed of our enemies who, according to MacDonald, "stand for the privileged class and desire to preserve it." It would seem that once we stand for the annihilation of a privileged class which has no desire to pass from the scene, we have therein the basic content of the class struggle. But no: MacDonald desires to "evoke" the consciousness of social solidarity. With whom? The solidarity of the working class is the expression of its internal welding in the struggle with the bourgeoisie. The social solidarity which MacDonald preaches is the solidarity of the exploited with the exploiters, in other words, the maintenance of exploitation. In addition to this, MacDonald boasts that his idea is distinct from the idea of our grandfathers: having in mind Karl Marx. In actuality MacDonald is distinguished from his "grandfathers" in this sense, that he has returned to his great-grandfathers. This ideological skilly which MacDonald puts out for a new school signifies—on an absolutely new historical base—a return to the petty bourgeois sentimental Socialism subjected by Marx to a devastating criticism even in 1847 and earlier.

To the class struggle MacDonald opposes the idea of the solidarity of all those virtuous elements who endeavour to reconstruct society by means of democratic reforms. In this presentation the struggle of the class is replaced by the "constructive" activity of a political party, which is formed not on a class basis but on the basis of social solidarity. These magnificent ideas of our grandfathers, Robert Owen, Weitling, and others, completely emasculated and made serviceable for parliamentary application, sound especially nonsensical in contemporary Britain, with its numerically powerful Labour Party based on the trade unions. There is not another country in the world where the class character of Socialism should be revealed so objectively, clearly, indisputably, and directly, by history as in Britain, for there the Labour Party grew out of the parliamentary representation of the trade unions, in other words, out of the purely class organisations of employed labour. When the Conservatives, and the Liberals for that matter, endeavour to prohibit the raising of political levies by the trade unions, they are not unsuccessfully opposing the idealist conception of MacDonald's party to the empirically class character which the party has taken on in Britain. It is true that there are a certain number of Fabian intelligentsia and Liberals who have come over to the party in despair, at the head of the Labour Party, but in the first place we must firmly hope that sooner or later the workers will sweep out this rubbish with a housebroom, and in the second place, even now those 4½ million votes given for the Labour Party are, with insignificant exceptions, the votes of the British workers. Still far from all of the workers vote for their own party. But it is the workers almost alone who do vote for the Labour Party.

This must not be taken to imply that the Fabians, I.L.P.ers, and Liberal deserters have no influence on the politics of the working class. On the contrary, their influence is extremely great, but it has no independent nature. In struggling against proletarian class-consciousness the reformists are in the last resort the instrument of the ruling class.

Throughout the whole history of the British Labour Movement is to be found the pressure of the bourgeoisie on the proletariat by means of radicals, intelligentsia, drawing-room and church socialists, Owenites, who reject the class struggle, put forward the principle of social solidarity, preach co-operation with the bourgeoisie, curb, enfeeble, and politically debase the proletariat. The programme of the Independent Labour Party shows in full correspondence with this "tradition" that the party "struggles to the uniting of the organised workers together with all people of all classes who believe in Socialism." This consciously diffuse formula has as its object the mollifying of the class character of Socialism. No one, of course, demands the complete closing of the doors of the party against the tested entrants from other classes. However, their number is even at present absolutely insignificant, if one does not confine oneself to statistics of the leading groups, but takes the party as a whole; and in the future, when the party takes the revolutionary road, it will become still less. But their formula of "people of all classes" is necessary to the I.L.P.ers in order to delude the workers in the matter of the actual class basis of their power, supplanting it with the fiction of super-class solidarity.

We recalled that many workers still vote for

bourgeois candidates. MacDonald grows wise and interprets this fact in the political interests of the bourgeoisie. "We must consider the worker not as a worker, but as a man," he teaches, and adds, "even Toryism has learnt to some extent to . . . treat people as people. Therefore many workers voted for Toryism." In other words, as the Conservatives, frightened by the pressure of the workers, have learnt to adapt themselves to the most backward of them, to disintegrate them, to delude them, to play on their darkest prejudices, and frighten them with false documents, this shows that the Tories know how to treat people as people!

The British Labour organisations most free from alloy in their class composition, that is, the trade unions, have lifted the Labour Party directly on to their backs. Therein the profound changes in the situation of Britain have found their expression—her weakening on the world market, the change in her economic structure, the falling away of the middle classes, the break-up of Liberalism. A class party is necessary to the proletariat, it endeavours with all its powers to create it, it brings pressure to bear on the trade unions, it pays political levies. But this increasing pressure from below, from the factories and workshops, from the docks and mines, is opposed with resistance from above, from the sphere of official British politics, with its national traditions of "love of freedom," of world predominance, of cultural primogeniture, of democracy and Protestant piety. If from all these component parts be prepared a political mixture (for the weakening of the class-consciousness of the British proletariat), the result is the Fabian programme.

MacDonald endeavours to declare openly that the

Labour Party based on the trade unions is a super-class organisation; but the "democratic" State of British capital has a still more super-class character for him. True, the present State, administrated by landowners, bankers, shipowners, and mining magnates, is not "complete" democracy. Certain imperfections still remain in it. "Democracy, and for example (!!) an industrial system not administrated by the people, are two incompatible conceptions. In other words, you have democracy, only a little damaged; the wealth created by the people belongs not to the people but to an insignificant minority of the people. Perhaps this is accidental? No, bourgeois democracy is a system of institutions and measures by the aid of which the needs and demands of the working masses, reaching ever higher, are neutralised, distorted, rendered innocuous, or are simply stultified. He lies who says that in Britain, France, the United States, and other democracies private ownership is maintained by the will of the people. No one ever asked the people about it. The workers are born and brought up under conditions not of their creating. The State school, the State Church, inoculate them with conceptions directed entirely to the maintenance of the existing order. Parliamentary democracy is only a résumé of this state of things. MacDonald's own party enters into this system as an indispensable element of its composition. When the course of events, usually of a catastrophic nature, such as great economic disturbances, crises, wars, make the social system unbearable to the workers, they have neither the possibility nor the desire to lead their revolutionary agitation into the channels of capitalist democracy. In other words: when the masses comprehend how long they have been deluded they carry out a revolution. A successful revolution tranfers the power to them, and the conquest of power enables them to construct a new State apparatus, answering to their interests.

But it is just this that MacDonald will not accept. "The revolution in Russia," he says, "taught us a great lesson. It showed that revolution is a ruin and a calamity, and nothing more." Here the reactionary Fabian stands before us in all his revolting nakedness. Revolution leads only to calamity! But the British democracy led to the imperialist war, and not only in the sense that all the capitalist States were generally responsible—no, in the sense of the direct and immediate responsibility of British diplomacy, consciously and calculatingly thrusting Europe into war. If the British "democracy" had declared that it would enter the war on the side of the Entente, Germany and Austria-Hungary would no doubt have withdrawn. But the British Government acted otherwise: it secretly promised support to the Entente, and calculatingly deluded Germany with the possibility of its neutrality. Thus British "democracy" deliberately led to the war, with the ruin of which the calamities of revolution cannot, of course, be compared in the very least. But in addition to this, what deaf ears and shameless face are necessary in order in the face of a revolution which overthrew Tsarism, nobility, and bourgeoisie, shook the Church, awakened to a new life a nation of 130 millions, a whole family of nations, to declare that revolution is a calamity and *nothing more.* Here also MacDonald repeats Baldwin. He has no knowledge or understanding either of the Russian revolution or of British history. We are constrained to remind him of that which we recalled to the mind of the Conservative Premier. If in the economic sphere the initiative belonged to Britain until the fourth quarter of the last century, so in the political sphere Britain developed during the last century and a half in large measure with the assistance of European and American revolutions. The great French revolution, and the July revolution of 1830, and the revolution of '48, and the North American civil war of the sixties, and the Russian revolution of 1905, and the Russian revolution of 1917, all pushed forward the social development of Great Britain and left their marks on her history in the signposts of the greatest legislative reforms. Without the Russian revolution of 1917 MacDonald would not have been Premier in 1924. It will be understood that we are not trying to claim that the MacDonald Ministry was the greatest conquest of October. But in any case it was in great measure its by-product. And even the children's books teach us that it is not wise to gnaw the roots of the oak-tree from which you are gathering acorns.

And, moreover, what senseless Fabian arrogance: as the Russian revolution has taught "us" (whom?) a lesson, "we" (who?) will arrange our affairs without a revolution. But why in that case did not all the preceding wars enable "you" to dispense with the imperialist war? Just as the bourgeoisie calls every succeeding war the last war, so MacDonald wishes to call the Russian revolution the last revolution. But why exactly should the British bourgeoisie give way to the British proletariat, and peacefully, without a struggle, renounce their own property, when they have previously received the firm assurance of MacDonald that after the experience of the Russian revolution the British Socialists will never go the way of violence? When and where did the ruling class ever yield power and property on the order of a peaceful vote—and especially such a class as the British bourgeoisie, which has behind it centuries of world rapacity.

MacDonald is against revolution, but in favour of organic evolution; he applies to society a badly digested biological conception. For him evolution, as the sum of accumulated partial changes, is comparable to the development of living organisms, the transformation of a chrysalis into a butterfly, and so on, while in this last process he ignores exactly the decisive critical moments, when the new being bursts from the old chrysalis in revolutionary wise. Here, too, in passing it is revealed that MacDonald is "for a revolution similar to that which took place within the womb of feudalism, when the industrial revolution came to maturity." Evidently, in his blatant ignorance, MacDonald conceives that the industrial revolution took place molecularly, without disturbance, without misfortune and devastation. He simply does not know the history of Britain (there is no point in mentioning the history of other countries), and, most of all, does not understand that the industrial revolution while it was still maturing within the womb of feudalism, in the form of trade capital, led to the Reformation, brought the Stuarts into conflict with Parliament, gave birth to the civil war, and ruined and devastated Britain, in order afterwards to enrich her.

It would be wearying to occupy ourselves here with the interpretation of the process of transformation of the chrysalis into the butterfly in order to get the necessary social analogies. It is simpler and shorter to recommend MacDonald to ponder over the old comparison of revolution with birth. Is it not possible to gain a "lesson" here, as well as from the Russian revolution? Since births give "nothing" but pains and misery (the child does not come into the reckoning !), in future the population is recommended to multiply in the painless Fabian fashion, availing themselves of the talents of Mrs. Snowden in the capacity of unqualified midwife.

We must point out none the less that the matter is not at all so simple. Even the chick, when formed inside the egg, must apply force to the calcareous prison enclosing it ; if some Fabian chick, out of Christian or other considerations, decided to refrain from violent activities, the calcareous envelope would inevitably suffocate it. British pigeon fanciers, by means of an artificial selection, achieve special varieties, with a continually shortening beak. But there comes a moment when the beak of a new stock is so short that the poor creature is unequal to breaking the egg-shell, and the young pigeon perishes, a sacrifice to compulsory restraint from revolutionary activities, and a stop is put to the further progress of varieties of short-bills. If our memory is not at fault, MacDonald can read about this in Darwin. Having entered upon MacDonald's favourite course of analogies with the organic world, one can say that the political art of the British bourgeoisie consists in shortening the revolutionary beak of the proletariat, and so not allowing him to pierce the shell of the capitalist State. The beak of the proletariat is its party. If we look at MacDonald, Thomas, Mr. and Mrs. Snowden, we have to confess that the work of the bourgeoisie in selecting short-billed and soft-billed has been crowned with astonishing success, for these individuals are not only not fit for the piercing of the capitalist shell, but indeed are not fit for anything.

Here, however, the analogy ends, revealing all the conditionality of this kind of hasty search in the primers of biology as a substitute for the study of the methods of historical development. Although human society grew out of the conditions of the organic and inorganic world, it presents them in such a complicated and concentrated blending that it demands an independent knowledge. Social organism is distinguished from biological organism by, among other things, a much greater flexibility, and by a capability of regrouping its elements, of conscious selection to a certain degree of its instruments and processes, of a conscious utilisation within certain limits of the experience of the past, and so on. The pigeon in the egg cannot change its too short beak, and so it perishes. The working class, confronted with the question—to be or not to be—can drive out the MacDonalds and Mrs. Snowdens and arm themselves with the beak of a revolutionary party for the destruction of the capitalist system.

Especially curious seems MacDonald's combination of a crude biological theory of society with an idealistic Christian hatred of materialism. "You talk of revolution, of catastrophic leaps, but look at nature, how intelligently a caterpillar acts when it has to transform itself into a chrysalis; observe the worthy tortoise, and you will find in its movement the natural rhythm of the transformation of society. Learn from nature!" And in the same breath MacDonald stigmatises materialism—"triviality, a senseless assertion, in it there is neither spiritual nor intellectual delicacy." . . . MacDonald and—delicacy! Is that not in very deed an amazing "delicacy": to seek for suggestions for the collective social activity of man in a caterpillar, and at the same time to demand an immortal soul with a comfortable existence after death for his own personal use?

"Socialists are accused of being poets. That is true," MacDonald explains. "We are poets. There cannot be good politics without poetry. In general there is nothing good without poetry." And so on in the same style. And in conclusion: "The world has need of some kind of political and social Shakespeare more than anything else." This twaddle about poetry is perhaps not so politically pernicious as conversations on the impermissibility of force. But MacDonald's complete mental bankruptcy is here expressed with still greater conviction, if possible. A sober and timorous curmudgeon, in whom there is as much poetry as in a square inch of felting, endeavours to dumbfound the world with Shakespearean grimaces. Here is where those "apish" tricks originally begin, which MacDonald tried to ascribe to the Bolsheviks.

MacDonald as the "poet" of Fabianism! The policy of Sidney Webb as an artistic creation! The Ministry of Thomas, as colonial poetry! And finally, the budget of Mr. Snowden as the song of triumphant love of the City of London!

In gabbling about a social Shakespeare, MacDonald overlooked Lenin. How well it is—for MacDonald, if not for Shakespeare—that the greatest of British poets was creating three centuries ago; MacDonald has had sufficient time in which to see the Shakespeare in Shakespeare. He would never have recognised him if he had been his contemporary. For MacDonald had overlooked—absolutely and completely overlooked—Lenin. A philistine blindness finds its double expression in aimless sighings after a Shakespeare and in the ignoring of his own greatest contemporary.

"Socialism is interested in art and the classics." It is amazing how this "poet" succeeds in vulgarising by his contact a thought in which of itself there is nothing vulgar. To be convinced of this it is sufficient to read the conclusion: "Even where great poverty and great unemployment exist, as, unfortunately, in our country, the citizens (?) must not begrudge the acquisition of pictures and in general of anything which evokes enthusiasm and uplifts the spirit of young and old." From this excellent counsel it is, however, not quite clear whether the acquisition of pictures is recommended to the unemployed themselves and whether it is proposed to make a corresponding supplementary assignation for their needs, or whether MacDonald counsels the high-born gentlemen and ladies to purchase pictures, "in spite of unemployment," and so "uplift their spirits." We must suppose that the second explanation is nearer the truth. But in that case do we not see before us a drawing-room Liberal, Protestant minister, who first says some tearful words on poverty and the "religion of the conscience," and afterwards invites his worldly flock not to give themselves over unduly to melancholy and to continue their former manner of life? Let who desires believe after this that materialism is triviality, while MacDonald is a social poet, yearning after Shakespeare. As for us, we think that if in the physical world there exists a degree of absolute cold, then in the mental world there must be a degree of absolute triviality—and that is the ideological temperature of MacDonald.

Sidney and Beatrice Webb represent another variety of Fabianism. They are accustomed to assiduous work, they know the value of facts and figures, and this sets a certain bound to the diffusiveness of their thought. They are not less boring than MacDonald, but they are sometimes more instructive, when they do not overstep the bounds of Fabian investigations. In the realm of generalisations they stand a little higher than MacDonald. At the Congress of the Labour Party in 1923 Sidney Webb called to mind that the founder of British Socialism was not Karl Marx but Robert Owen, who preached not the class war, but the time-hallowed doctrine of the brotherhood of all humanity. Until the present day Webb continues to consider John Stuart Mill the classic of political economy, and in accordance with this, teaches that the struggle must be carried on not between capital and labour, but between the overwhelming majority of the nation and the expropriators of rent. This alone is sufficient to characterise the theoretic level of the chief economist of the Labour Party! As is well known, even in Britain the historical process does not go on in accordance with Webb. Trade unions represent an organisation of employed labour against capital. On the basis of the trade unions the Labour Party has grown up and even made Sidney Webb a Minister. He fulfilled his programme only in the sense that he did not carry on a struggle against the expropriators of surplus values. But neither did he carry it on against the expropriators of rent.

In 1923 the Webbs published a book entitled the *Decay of Capitalist Civilisation.*[1] In its essentials the book represents a partly diluted, partly renovated, paraphrase of the old commentaries of Kautsky on the Erfurt programme. But in addition in the *Decay of Capitalist Civilisation* the political tendency of Fabianism is expressed in all its hopelessness, this time half consciously. That the capitalist system must be transformed, say the Webbs, there is no doubt.

[1] London: George Allen & Unwin Ltd.

(For whom ?) But the whole question is, How will it be transformed ? "It may by considerate adaptation be made to pass gradually and peacefully into a new form." For this not much is necessary: good will from both sides. "Unfortunately," the estimable authors relate, agreement is not reached on the question how to replace the capitalist system, for "many" consider that the elimination of private ownership is tantamount to the cessation of the rotation of the earth on its axis. "But they misunderstand the position." There now, how unfortunately the matter is arranged. All might be fixed up to universal satisfaction by way of "considerate adaptation," if only the workers and capitalists identically understood what is necessary and how it is necessary. But since "so far" this has not been achieved, the capitalists vote for the Conservatives. And the deduction ? At this point our poor Fabians are beaten altogether, and here the "decay of capitalism" is transformed into a tearful "decay of Fabianism." "Before the great war there seemed to be a substantial measure of consent," the book relates, "that the present-day social order had to be gradually changed, in the direction of greater equality," and so on. Who gave their consent ? Where did they give their consent ? These people take their own little Fabian ant-hillock for the world. "We thought, perhaps wrongly (!) that this characteristic British acquiescence on the part of a limited governing class in the rising claims" of the people would continue and lead to a peaceful transformation of society. But after the war everything was set back : the conditions of existence of the working masses worsened, we are threatened with the restoration of the *veto* of a strong second chamber (the House of Lords), with the special purpose of resisting further concessions to the workers, and so on. What deduction is made from that? It was in the hopeless search of a conclusion that the Webbs wrote their book. Its concluding phrase is: "In an attempt, *possibly vain*, to make the parties understand their problem and each other better . . . we offer this little book." Surely that is magnificent: a "little book" as the means of reconciling the proletariat with the bourgeoisie! We recapitulate: until the war, "it seemed," it was generally recognised that the present system must be changed for the better; however, there was not complete agreement on the character of the change; the capitalists stood for private ownership, the workers, against; after the war the objective situation worsened, and the political divergence became still more pronounced; *therefore* the Webbs write a book in the hope of disposing both sides to a reconciliation; but that hope is "possibly vain." Yes, possibly, very possibly. These worthy Webbs, who have such faith in the strength of conviction, in our opinion ought in the interests of "gradualness" to have set themselves for a beginning a more simple task, as, for example, that of convincing certain highly placed Christian good-for-nothings to renounce their monopolistic trade in opium and the poisoning of millions of people in the East.

Poor, miserable, silly Fabianism, ignominious in its intellectual difficulties!

To endeavour to sort over the other philosophical varieties of Fabianism would be an absolutely hopeless business, since among these people "freedom of opinion" reigns in the sense that every one of the leaders has his own personal philosophy, which in the final account is made up of all these same reactionary elements of Conservatism, Liberalism, Protestantism, but in somewhat different combinations. Not so very long ago we were extremely surprised when Bernard Shaw, who it would seem is so keen-witted and so critical a writer, informed us that Marx had long since been superseded by the great work of Wells on universal history.[1] That such revelations should come completely unexpected by all humanity is explained by the fact that the Fabians in their theoretic relationships present an amazingly circumscribed little world, profoundly provincial, although they live in London. Their philosophic imaginings are unnecessary, of course, either to the Conservatives or to the Liberals. Still less necessary are they to the working class, to whom they give nothing and explain nothing. These labours in the end serve only to explain to the Fabians themselves for what purpose Fabianism exists in the world. Together with theological literature, it is perhaps the most useless and in any case the most boring form of verbal creation.

In various circles in Britain they speak at the moment with a certain contempt of the people of the "Victorian era," that is to say, of the men of affairs of Queen Victoria's times. In Britain everything has passed on from those times, but perhaps the Fabian type has been best preserved. The cheaply optimistic Victorian epoch, when it seemed that to-morrow would be a little better than to-day, and the day after to-morrow still better than to-morrow, found its most

[1] I confess that until Bernard Shaw's letter I did not even know of the existence of this book. I then made its acquaintance. I cannot with clear conscience say that I read it through, for acquaintance with two or three chapters was quite sufficient to avoid a further waste of time. Conceive a complete absence of method, of historical perspective, of understanding of the mutual dependence of various sides of social life, and absence of any kind of scientific discipline in general, and imagine, further, that the "historian," overstocked with these qualities, with the careless mien of a man finishing his Sunday walk, wanders to and fro and up and down through the history of several tens of thousands of years. You will then have Wells's book, which is to replace the Marxist school.

finished expression in the Webbs, Snowden, MacDonald, and other Fabians. Hence it is that they seem such awkward and unnecessary survivals of an epoch which has suffered a final and irrevocable overthrow. One can say without exaggeration that the Fabian Society, founded in 1884 for the purpose of "awakening the social conscience," is to-day the most reactionary group of people in Great Britain. Neither the Conservative Club nor Oxford University, neither the Anglican episcopate nor other clerical institutions, can bear any kind of comparison with the Fabians. All these are institutions of the hostile classes, and the revolutionary movement of the proletariat will inevitably burst through their dam. But the proletariat is held in check by just these groups who are their directing upper circles, in other words, by the Fabian politicians and their choral accompaniments. These bombastic authorities, pedants, arrogant and ranting poltroons, systematically poison the Labour Movement, befog the consciousness of the proletariat, and paralyse its will. Only thanks to them do Toryism, Liberalism, the Church, the monarchy, the aristocracy and the bourgeoisie continue to retain their hold and even to feel that they are firmly in the saddle. The Fabians, the I.L.P.ers, the conservative bureaucrats of the trade unions represent at the moment the most counter-revolutionary force of Great Britain, and perhaps of all the world's development. The overthrow of the Fabians will mean the liberation of the revolutionary energy of the British proletariat, which will mean the conquest for Socialism of the British fortress of reaction, the liberation of India and Egypt, and the giving of a mighty impetus to the movement and development of the nations of the East. In rejecting force, the Fabians believe only in the might of "ideas." If the healthy seed be separated from this insipid and hypocritical philosophy it leads to this conclusion, that not any regime can maintain itself by force alone. This has reference to the regime of British imperialism also. In a country where an overwhelming majority of the population is made up of the proletariat, the ruling Conservative-Liberal imperialist clique could not maintain itself for one day if those means of force they have in their hands were not strengthened, and added to, and smeared over with pseudo-socialist ideas, thus misleading and splitting up the proletariat.

The French educationalists of the eighteenth century saw the chief enemy in Catholicism, in clericalism, in the priesthood, and reckoned that it was necessary to throttle the vermin before it would be possible to move forward. They were right in this sense, that it was the priesthood, the organised regime of superstition, the Catholic spiritual gendarmerie, that stood athwart the road of bourgeois society, damming the development of science, art, political ideas, and economics. Fabianism, MacDonaldism, Pacifism plays at the moment a similar rôle in relation to the historical movement of the proletariat. It is the chief rallying point of British imperialism and of the European, if not the world, bourgeoisie. At any cost, these self-satisfied pedants, these gabbling eclectics, these sentimental careerists, these upstart liveried lackeys of the bourgeoisie must be shown in their natural form to the workers. To reveal them as they are will mean their hopeless discrediting. To discredit them will mean the performing of a great service for the historical process. On that day when the British proletariat is cleansed of the mental abomination of Fabianism, humanity, and in the first place Europe, will be immediately increased in stature by a whole head.

V

THE QUESTION OF REVOLUTIONARY FORCE

[*Popularly expounded, to suit the intelligence not only of the most backward workers, but even of certain of the less hopeless leaders.*]

WE have acquainted ourselves with MacDonald's views on revolutionary force. They were shown to be a development of Mr. Baldwin's Conservative theory of gradualness. The rejection of force by the " left wing " Lansbury bears a more curious, though more sincere, character. He, do you see, just simply " does not believe " in force. He " does not believe " in either a capitalistic army or an armed uprising. If he believed in force he would not vote, he says, for the British fleet, but would join the Communists. There's a brave for you ! That Lansbury, who does not believe in force, believes in life after death, does doubtful honour of course to his sense of realistic penetration. None the less, with all due respect for Mr. Lansbury, certain events have occurred on the earth by the aid of force. Whether Lansbury believes or not in the British war fleet, the Indians know that that fleet exists. In April 1919 the British General O'Dwyer gave orders to fire without previous warning on an unarmed Indian meeting in Amritsar, as a result of which 450 persons were killed, and 1,500 wounded. While we may leave the dead in peace, in any case it has to be said of the wounded that they cannot "not believe" in force. But even in his capacity as a believing Christian, Lansbury should have considered that if in their day the crafty rogues of Jewish priests with the cowardly Roman pro-consul Pilate, the political ancestor of MacDonald, had not applied force to Christ, there would not have been either the acceptance of the torturing crown, or the resurrection, or the ascension; and Mr. Lansbury himself would not have been afforded the opportunity of being born a pious Christian and becoming a bad Socialist. Not believing in force is the same as not believing in gravitation. All life is ordered on various forms of force, on the balancing of one force with another, and the renunciation of liberating force means the support of the oppressing force governing the world to-day.

We feel, however, that nothing can be achieved by means of fleeting observations at this juncture. The question of force and its "rejection" by the gentlemen Pacifists, Christian Socialists, and other bigots, occupies such a large place in British politics, that it demands from us a special and detailed consideration, applicable to the political level of the present "leaders" of the British Labour Party. And we apologise in advance to our other readers for this level.

What actually is meant by the rejection of any kind of force? If, let us suppose, a thief were to break into the house of Mr. Lansbury, we are very afraid that that devout gentleman (we are speaking now of the head of the home) would use force or call the nearest policeman for that purpose. Even if out of his merciful heart Lansbury were to let the thief go in peace (of which we are not at all sure), then it would be only under the condition, quite understandable of itself, that he immediately left the house. And the worthy gentleman can allow himself the luxury of such a Christian gesture only because his house is under the protection of the British laws of property and of their innumerable Arguses, so that broadly speaking nightly visits of thieves are the exception rather than the rule. If Lansbury attempts to answer us by saying that breaking into a respectable private Christian house is force, and thus causes the necessity of resistance, we shall tell him that such reasoning is a complete abjuration of the rejection of force ; on the contrary, it is its recognition both in principle and in practice, and may be transferred in its entirety to the class struggle, where the daily invasion of the thief-capitalist into the life and labour of the proletariat and the expropriation of surplus value completely justifies resistance. Maybe Lansbury will answer that by force he understands not all measures of compulsion in general, without which our excellent social life cannot be carried on, but only the breaking of the sixth commandment, which has laid down : " Thou shalt not kill." In justification of such an enunciation of the question many bombastic phrases about the sanctity of human life may be brought forward. But here we must ask in the language of the gospel parables, which is the most intelligible to the leaders of British Socialism, how will Mr. Lansbury act in the event of a robber raising a stick to children in his very sight, if there be no means of saving them other than an immediate and well-aimed shot from a revolver ? If our supposititious interlocutor has no desire to occupy himself with such absolutely mean sophisms, he will perhaps for his own peace of mind answer that our example bears too exceptional a character. But that answer will only signify all the same that Lansbury has entrusted his right of resort to murder in suitable circumstances to his police, the specialised organisation of force, thus in the majority of cases relieving himself of the need to use a revolver or even to ponder on the purpose for which it is designed.

But what is to happen, we ask, if armed strike-breakers injure or kill strikers? Such events are quite customary in America, and even in other countries they are not unusual. The workers cannot entrust their right to resist strike-breakers to the police, for in all countries the police defend the right of the strike-breakers to injure and kill the strikers, to whom as is well known the law of the sanctity of human life is not extended. We ask, have the strikers any right to use sticks, stones, revolvers, bombs, against Fascists, the Ku-Klux-Klan bands, and other hired scoundrels of capital? Here is a tiny little question, to which we would request a clear and definite answer, one in no way evasive or hypocritical. If Lansbury tells us that the task of Socialism is to give the popular masses such an education that the Fascists should cease to be Fascists, the scoundrels to be scoundrels, and so on, his answer will be the purest hypocrisy. It is absolutely unchallenged that the aim of Socialism is to eliminate force, first of all in its most crude and bloody forms, and afterwards in other more concealed forms. But we are discussing not the character and morals of the future Communist society, but the concrete ways and means of the struggle with capitalistic force. When Fascists disorganise strikes, capture the editorial staff of a newspaper or a cashbox, injure or kill workers' representatives, while the police encircle the burglars with a ring of inviolability, only the most corrupted hypocrite could counsel the workers not to answer with blow for blow under the pretext that in the Communist society there will not be room for force. It goes without saying that in every given case it is necessary to decide, in relation to all the circumstances, how to answer the enemy and *to what limits* to go in resistance. But this is a question of a tactical expediency, which has nothing in common with the recognition or denial in principle of force.

What strictly speaking is force? Where does it begin? Where do the permissible and expedient collective actions of the mass pass over into force? We greatly doubt whether Lansbury or anybody else from among the Pacifists is capable of giving an answer to this question, unless they confine themselves to a simple reliance on the criminal code, where it is stated what is allowed and what is not allowed. The class struggle is a continual sequence of open or masked forces, which are "regulated" in more or less degree by the State, which in turn represents the organised apparatus of force of the stronger of the antagonists, in other words, the ruling class. Is a strike resort to force? There was a time when strikes were forbidden, and every strike was almost inevitably accompanied by physical conflicts. Then, as the result of the development of the strike struggle, in other words, as the result of the violent onslaught of the masses on the law, or, to be more exact, as the result of the continual blows of the masses upon the lawful force, strikes were legalised. Does that mean that Lansbury regards only peaceful, "legal" strikes, i.e. those permitted by the bourgeoisie, as permissible methods of struggle? But if the workers had not organised strikes in the beginning of the nineteenth century, the British bourgeoisie would not have legalised them in 1824. If one allows the application of force or violence in the form of strikes, one must accept all the consequences, among others the defence of the strikes from strike-breakers with the assistance of well-directed measures of counter force.

Further, if strikes of the workers against capitalists or separate groups of capitalists are permissible, does Lansbury venture to avow that a general strike of workers against a Fascist Government which is suppressing workers' unions, breaking up the workers' press, flooding the ranks of workers with provocateurs and murderers, is impermissible? And again, a general strike cannot be declared on what day you like and what time you like, but only under definite and concrete conditions. But that is a question of strategic expediency, and not one of a general "moral" value. As for a general strike as one of the most decisive methods of struggle, Lansbury and his adherents taken altogether are not likely to think out another method which the proletariat could adopt for the reaching of decisive ends. But in actuality Lansbury does not abase himself to the extent of recommending the workers to wait until the spirit of brotherly love reigns in the hearts of the Italian Fascists, shall we say, who, it is to the point to mention, are many of them devout Catholics. But if it be recognised that the workers have not only the right, but also the duty to prepare themselves for a general strike against the Fascist regime, we must draw the logical conclusions from that recognition. A general strike, if it is not to be a mere demonstration, implies a tremendous upheaval of society, and in any case puts to hazard the fate of a political regime and the reputation of the revolutionary class force. One may undertake a general strike only when the working class, and, in the first place, its advance-guard, are prepared to carry the struggle through to the end. But neither does Fascism intend to yield in face of some form of peaceful strike manifestation. In the case of a real and immediate danger the Fascists will set in motion all their forces, will put in action provocations, murders, and incendiarism on an unprecedented scale. One asks: are the leaders of the general strike to be allowed to form their own troops for the defence of the strikers from violence, and for the disarming and demoralisation of the Fascist bands? And as no one has ever succeeded, at any rate within our memory, in disarming infuriated enemies with the aid of religious hymns, it is evident that the revolutionary bands must be armed with revolvers and hand grenades, until they succeed in gaining possession of rifles, machine guns, and cannon. Or perhaps it is at this point that the realm of impermissible violence begins? But then we are completely lost in a maze of nonsensical and shameful inconsistencies. Any general strike which does not safeguard itself against force and break-up is a demonstration of cowardliness, and is foredoomed to defeat. Only a madman or a traitor will sound the call to struggle under such conditions. An "unarmed" strike struggle will, owing to the logic of relationships which are not dependent on Lansbury, evoke armed conflicts. This very often takes place in economic strikes; it is absolutely unavoidable in a revolutionary political strike, so long as the strike has as aim the overthrow of a particular regime. Whoever renounces force should renounce all struggles generally, in other words, he should really stand in the partisan ranks of the triumphant forces of the ruling classes.

But the matter does not end there. We point out that the hypothetical general strike has as its aim the overthrow of a Fascist Government. That can be attained only by overcoming its armed forces. But here again two roads are conceivable: a direct military victory over the forces of reaction, or their attraction to the side of revolution. Neither one of these two ways is realisable in its simple form. Revolutionary insurrection will gain the victory in that case where it succeeds in breaking up the firmest, most determined, and most dependable divisions of reaction, and in attracting to its side the remaining armed forces of the regime. Again, that can only be attained in conditions where the wavering governmental soldiers become convinced that the working masses are not simply demonstrating their dissatisfaction, but are absolutely determined to overthrow the Government this time at whatever the cost, not hesitating before the most ruthless measures of struggle. Only by giving that kind of impression to the wavering troops will it be possible to throw them on to the side of the people. The more procrastinating, vacillating, and compromising the policy of the leaders of the general strike, the less wavering will there be in the soldiers' ranks, the more determinedly will they support the existing authority, and the more chances will the latter have of coming out victors from the crisis, in order afterwards to let loose all the scorpions of bloody repression on the heads of the working class. In other words, once the working class is compelled to take to a general political strike as a means of gaining its freedom, it must take account beforehand of the fact that the strike will inevitably give rise to partial and general, armed and semi-armed conflicts; it must take account beforehand of the fact that the strike will not be defeated only in so far as it is able immediately to put up the necessary resistance to strike-breakers, provocateurs, Fascists, and such-like. It must foresee that the Government whose fate is in the balance will at some moment or other of the struggle inevitably order

its armed forces into the streets, and that on the outcome of the clash of the revolutionary masses with this armed force hangs the destiny of the existing regime, and consequently of the proletariat. The workers must in advance take all measures to draw the soldiers to the side of the people by means of preliminary agitation ; but at the same time it must foresee that the Government will always be left with a sufficient number of dependable or semi-dependable soldiers for them to call out for the purpose of quelling the insurrection ; and, consequently, in the final resort the question has to be decided by an armed conflict, for which it is necessary to prepare with all systematisation, and which it is necessary to carry on with all revolutionary determination.

In the revolutionary struggle only the greatest determination is of avail to strike the arms out of the hands of reaction, to limit the period of civil war, and to lessen the number of its victims. If this course be not taken it is better not to take to arms at all. If arms are not resorted to, it is impossible to organise a general strike ; if the general strike is renounced, there can be no thought of any serious struggle. Then there remains only to educate the workers in the spirit of complete prostration, which the official school directing the party, the clergy of all the churches, and . . . the socialistic proclaimers of the impermissibility of violence, already do.

But this one thing is worthy of note : just as in practical life the philosophic idealists feed themselves with bread, meat, and, indeed, with all kinds of contemptible matter, and, without reckoning on their immortal souls, endeavour to avoid falling under an automobile, so the gentlemen pacifists, the spineless opponents of force, and moral idealists, appeal to the police force, and directly or indirectly avail themselves of it in those cases which come within the sphere of their immediate interests. As Mr. Lansbury is evidently not without some semblance of an emotional temperament, such happenings occur with him more often than with others. In the parliamentary debates on the question of unemployment (session of House of Commons March 9th) Lansbury recalled that the Unemployed Insurance Act in its present form was introduced in 1920 " not so much to preserve the lives of the men and their families, but, as Lord Derby had recently told them, to prevent revolution. In 1920 the whole of the ex-service men were taken in because the then Government was not quite sure whether they might not have turned their guns in a direction which the Government did not desire " (*The Times*, March 10, 1925). After these words the parliamentary report notes: " Opposition cheers," i.e. from the Labour Party; and cries of " Oh! " from the ministerial benches. Lansbury does not believe in revolutionary force. But none the less, following in the steps of Lord Derby, he recognises that the fear of revolutionary force gave birth to the Act for State insurance of unemployed. Lansbury carries on a fight against those who attempt to alter this law; therefore he believes that the law brought into being by fear of revolutionary force brings a certain gain to the working class. But by that fact is proved almost mathematically the value of revolutionary force. For, with all due respect to Mr. Lansbury, if there were no force there would not be any fear of it. If there were not a real possibility (and necessity) in certain cases of turning arms against the Government, that Government would have no foundation for being afraid of it.

Therefore Mr. Lansbury's so-called unbelief in force is the purest misapprehension. In actuality he makes use of this force, at any rate in the form of an argument, every day. Still more does he avail himself of the conquests of revolutionary force of the past decades and centuries. He refuses only to think it out to its logical conclusion. He renounces revolutionary force for the seizure of power, in other words for the complete liberation of the proletariat. But he lives in excellent harmony with force, and avails himself of it in any struggle which does not extend beyond the framework of bourgeois society. Mr. Lansbury is in favour of retail force and against wholesale force. He is like a vegetarian who could reconcile himself with equanimity to the flesh of ducks and rabbits, but who recoils with holy indignation from the slaughter of larger animals.

We foresee, however, that Mr. Lansbury, and those more diplomatic and hypocritical who think with him, will object : yes, against a Fascist regime, and in general against a despotic Government, force may be, and in the final account—we will not on the whole challenge the statement—is to a certain degree allowable ; but it is absolutely impermissible in a democratic regime. We, for our part, immediately register that objection as a surrender of the principal position, for in the beginning we were discussing not under what political conditions force is allowable or expedient, but whether it was permissible at all from a certain abstract humanitarian-Christian-Socialist point of view.

When we are told that revolutionary force is impermissible only in a regime of political democracy, then the whole question is lifted on to another plane. That does not mean, however, that the democratic opponents of force have more depth and wisdom than the Christian-humanitarian ones. We shall immediately be convinced without difficulty that this is not so.

In actual fact, is it true that the question of the expediency and permissibility of revolutionary force is decided by the more or less " democraticalness " of the *form* of bourgeois rule ? Such an enunciation of the case is completely refuted by historical experience. The struggle between the revolutionary and the pacific, legalistic, reformistic direction within the Labour Movement does not at all begin from the moment of the institution of a republic or the introduction of universal electoral rights. In the period of Chartism and right down to 1868 the workers in Britain were completely deprived of electoral rights, in other words, of the basic instruments of " peaceful " development. Yet the Chartist movement was broken between the partisans of physical force, who had the masses behind them, and the partisans of moral force, preponderating in petty-bourgeois intellectuals and worker-aristocrats. In Hohenzollern Germany, with an impotent Parliament, a struggle went on within the ranks of social-democracy between the partisans of parliamentary reform and the preachers of a revolutionary general strike. Finally, even in Tsarist Russia, under the regime of June 3rd, the Mensheviks liquidated the revolutionary methods of struggle under cover of the slogan of struggle for legality. Thus the appeal to a bourgeois republic or to universal suffrage, as a basic reformist and legalist argument, is the product of theoretical limitations, a short memory, or just simply hypocrisy. In its essentials legalist reformism implies the submission of the slaves to the institutions and laws of the slave-owners. Whether universal suffrage is part of these institutions or not, whether more they emphasise their independence of the proletarian organisations, the more they fall into slavery to the capitalist organisations. One may say without difficulty beforehand that in the measure of its inevitable displacement from, the trade unions and the Labour Party, Fabianism will more and more blend its fate with that of the intermediate elements of the industrial, commercial, and State-bureaucratic apparatus. After its present temporary exaltation, the Independent Labour Party will be inevitably thrown down, and, having become the "third party in industry," will get entangled in the legs of capital and labour.

VIII

PROSPECTS

Arising out of the fact that Mrs. Lloyd George, the wife of the former Premier, lost a valuable necklace, the *Daily Herald*, the organ of the Labour Party, meditated on the Liberal leaders, who go over to the side of the enemy and present their wives with valuable necklaces. The leader-writer of the paper came to the following instructive conclusion on this matter: " The existence of the Labour Party depends on its success in restraining the workers' leaders from following this same disastrous road." Arthur Ponsonby, a hopeless Liberal, who even in the ranks of the Labour Party has not ceased to be a Liberal, in the same number of the paper gives himself over to reflections on how the Liberal leaders, Asquith and Lloyd George, ruined the great Liberal Party. " Yes," the leader-writer repeats after him, " the Liberal leaders have changed their simple habits and manners for the manner of life of the wealthy with whom they continually associate ; they have assimilated arrogance in reference to the lower orders," and so on. One would have thought that there was nothing astonishing in the fact that Liberal leaders, in other words, one of the two bourgeois parties, lead the bourgeois manner of life. But for the Liberals in the Labour Party, Liberalism is represented as an abstract system of high ideas, and Liberal Ministers who buy their wives necklaces are represented as traitors to the ideas of Liberalism. The reflection on how to save the workers' leaders from following this disastrous road is, however, more instructive. It is absolutely clear that these considerations are timid and stammering warnings to the semi-Liberal Labour leaders on the part of the semi-Liberal Labour journalists, who have to reckon with the mood of its working-class readers. One can without difficulty imagine the careerist depravity which rules among the ministerial upper ten of the Labour Party! It is enough to mention that Mrs. Lloyd George herself, in a letter of protest to the editor of the *Daily Herald*, alluded to certain facts, in the nature of the "royal" gift received by MacDonald from his capitalist friend. After these reminiscences the editorship immediately shut up. It is miserable childishness to think that the conduct of the leaders of the Labour Party might be regulated with the aid of moralising stories about the necklaces of Mrs. Lloyd George, as if politics generally can be directed with the aid of abstract moral prescriptions. On the contrary, the morale of a class, its party, and its leaders, derive from politics, using the word in its broadest historical sense. This is nowhere more visible than in the very organisations of the British working class. The *Daily Herald* thought its way through to the perniciousness of association with the bourgeoisie for the worldly morals of the "leaders." But this, of course, depends entirely on the *political* relations with the bourgeoisie. If they stand on the principle of an irreconcilable class struggle, there will be no room for any kind of fraternisation; the workers' leaders will not yearn towards the bourgeois milieu, nor will the bourgeoisie accept them into their midst. But then the leaders of the Labour Party defend the idea of the co-operation of the classes and the rapprochement of their leaders. "Co-operation and mutual confidence between employers and workers," so for instance taught Mr. Snowden at one of the parliamentary sessions of the present year, "is an essential condition of the well-being of the country." We hear similar speeches from Clynes, the Webbs, and all the other lights. The leaders of the trade unions hold the same point of view; we hear from them only of the necessity of frequent meetings of employers' and workers' representatives at the common table. Meanwhile the policy of continual "friendly" association of the labour leaders with the bourgeois men of affairs in search of a common ground, in other words, the setting aside of that which distinguishes the one from the other, represents, as we learnt from the *Daily Mail*, a danger not only to the morals of the leaders, but also to the development of the party. What is to be done? When John Burns betrayed the working class, he began to say: "I have no desire for a special workers' point of view, as I have no desire for the workers' boots and the workers' margarine." That John Burns, having become a bourgeois Minister, in this way greatly improved his butter and his boots, is beyond question. But the evolution of Burns hardly improved the boots of the docker workers, who had raised Burns on their backs. Morals derive from politics. In order that Snowden's budget should be satisfactory to the city it was necessary that Snowden himself should come closer both in personal and in moral relationships to the bank directors than to the coalminers of Wales. And how does the matter stand with Thomas? We have told above of the banquet of the railway magnates, at which Thomas, the Secretary of the National Union of Railwaymen, swore that his soul belonged, not to the working class, but to "truth," and that in the search after this truth he, Thomas, had come to the banquet. It is noteworthy, none the less, that while all this abomination is narrated in detail in *The Times*, there is not one word in the *Daily Herald*. The unfortunate little paper occupies itself with moralising into space. Try to restrain the Thomases with parables on the necklace of Mrs. Lloyd George! Nothing comes of it. The Thomases must be expelled. But in order to do this it is necessary not to pass over in silence the banquet and other embraces of Thomas with the enemy, but to cry aloud of them, to denounce them, and to call the workers to a ruthless cleansing of their own ranks. In order to change the morality it is necessary to change the politics.

At this moment, as I write these lines (April 1925), despite the Conservative Government, the official politics of Britain stand under the sign of compromise: there must be "co-operation" between both industrial parties, there must be mutual concessions, the workers must become participants in this or that form in the receipts of industry, and so on. In this mental attitude of the Conservatives is expressed both the strength and the weakness of the British proletariat. It has compelled the Conservatives to adopt a policy of "reconciliation" owing to the creation of its own party. But it still permits the Conservatives to hope for "reconciliation," since it leaves MacDonald, Thomas, and company at the head of the Labour Party.

Baldwin delivers speech after speech on the indispensability of mutual forebearance if the country is to emerge from the difficulties of its present situation without *catastrophe*. The workers' "leader," Robert

Smillie, expresses his complete satisfaction with the speech: "What a remarkable call to forebearance on both sides!" Smillie promises wholly to follow the call. He hopes that the captains of industry also will take a more humane course in reference to the demand of the workers. "This is a wholly lawful and understandable desire," the leading paper *The Times* declares with a most serious mien. And all these mawkish speeches are made in the face of conditions of commercial and industrial difficulties, chronic unemployment, the handing of British orders for ship construction to Germany, and threatening conflicts in a whole series of industries—and where?—in Britain, with its experience of class struggles. In very truth a short memory of the working masses, and an unexampled hypocrisy of the rulers! The historical memory of the bourgeoisie is in its traditions of rulership, in the institutions, in the laws of the country, in the accumulated art of administration. The memory of the working class is in its party. A reformist party is a party of short memories.

If the compromise of the Conservatives is hypocrisy, it is compelled by serious causes. In the centre of the efforts of the governing parties of Europe stands at the moment the care for the maintenance of external and internal peace. The so-called "reaction" against war and the methods of the first post-war period are explained not at all by psychological causes. The capitalist regime showed itself sufficiently powerful and elastic in the time of war to call into being the special *illusions of war capitalism.* A bold centralised direction of economic life, the military seizure of inadequate economic values, a life in debt, the unlimited issue of paper money, the setting aside of social dangers with the aid of bloody violence on the one hand, and all possible sops on the other,—it seemed in the heat of the moment that these methods would settle all problems and overcome all difficulties. But economic activity speedily clipped the wings of the illusions of war capitalism. Germany went down to the very extreme of poverty. The wealthy French State does not emerge from its hardly concealed bankruptcy. The British State is compelled to maintain an army of unemployed almost twice the size of France's military army. The wealth of Europe has been shown to be in no way boundless. The continuation of wars and disturbances would mean the inevitable destruction of European capitalism. Hence the care for the "bringing into order" of relations between States and classes. The British Conservatives intelligently played on the fear of disturbances during the last election and won. Having come to power, they present themselves as the party of reconciliation, compromise, and social benevolence. "Safety, that is the key to the position"—these words of the Liberal Lord Grey are repeated by the Conservative Austen Chamberlain. The British Press of both bourgeois camps takes up the refrain. The tendency of struggle towards pacification, the creation of "normal" conditions, the safeguarding of a stable currency, the renewal of commercial agreements, will not of themselves settle one of the inconsistencies which led to the imperialist war, and are still more intensified by it. But only by beginning with this tendency and the political groupings being built up on it can one understand the present course of internal and external politics of the governing parties of Europe.

There is no need to say that these pacific tendencies come up against the opposition of post-war economics at every step. The British Conservatives have already begun to undermine the unemployed insurance law. It is impossible to make British industry *as she is at present* more capable of competition in any other way than by the lowering of the workers' wages. But this is not achievable while the present insurance of unemployed is retained, for it intensifies the strength of resistance of the working class. Advance post skirmishes have already begun over this ground. They can lead to serious struggles. In any case, in this sphere as in others the Conservatives will very quickly be compelled to speak with their own natural voice. The upper ten of the Labour Party will consequently be placed in a more and more difficult position.

It is quite in place here to recall those relationships which were established in the House of Commons after the 1906 elections, when a large labour faction first appeared on the parliamentary arena. During the first two years the labour representatives were surrounded with special attentions. But in the third year relations considerably worsened. In 1910 Parliament already "ignored" the labour faction. That was not the result of any irreconcilableness on the part of the latter, but resulted from the fact that outside Parliament the labour masses became more and more insistent. Having elected a large number of representatives, they expected serious changes in their own destiny. This expectation was one of the factors that prepared the way for the mighty strike movement of 1911–1913.

From this inquiry emerge certain deductions for the present moment. The more determined the pressure of the workers on their party, on capital, and on Parliament, the more inevitably will the frolicing of the Baldwin majority with the labour faction necessarily be transmuted into its converse. We have already spoken of this in connection with the question of the rôle of democracy and of revolutionary force in mutual relations between classes. Now we desire to approach this question from the point of view of the *internal development of the Labour Party itself.*

The directing rôle in the British Labour Party is played, as is well known, by the leaders of the Independent Labour Party, with MacDonald at the head. Not only before, but during the war, the Independent Labour Party took up a pacifist position, " condemned " social-imperialism, and in general belonged to the centrist tendency. The programme of the Independent Labour Party is directed " against militarism in any of its forms." At the end of the war the Independent Labour Party left the ranks of the Second International. On the resolution of the 1920 conference the Independents even entered into dealings with the Third International, and put it twelve questions, each more profound in thought than the other. The seventh question read: " Can Communism and the dictatorship of the proletariat be established only by armed force, or are parties which leave this question open allowed to join the Third International ? " A highly instructive picture: a butcher is armed with a jagged knife, and the lamb leaves the question open. None the less, in that critical period the Independent Labour Party raised the question of entering the Communist International, whereas now it excludes Communists from the Labour Party. The inconsistencies between the yesterday of the Independent Labour Party and the present policy of the Labour Party, especially in those months when they were in office, strikes one in the eye. And even to-day the policy of the Fabians in the Independent Labour Parry is distinguished from the policy of those same Fabians in the Labour Party. In these inconsistencies is to be found a faint echo of the struggle between the tendencies of centralism and social-imperialism. In MacDonald himself these tendencies are interwoven, with the consequence that the Christian pacifist builds light cruisers, in expectation of the time when it will be necessary to build heavy ones.

The chief features of socialist centralism are vagueness and indefiniteness of thought, compromise, and mediocrity. It will hang on so long as it is not forced to answer at the last moment the basic questions set before it. In a peaceful "organic" epoch centrism may maintain itself as the official doctrine of even a large and active Labour Party, as was the case with German social democracy before the war, for in that period the basic problems of State existence were not dependent on the decision of the proletarian party. But in general centralism has been most appropriate to small organisations, which by the very inadequacy of their influence are absolved from the necessity of giving a clear answer to all the questions of politics, and from carrying practical responsibility for such an answer. Just such was the centralism of the Independent Labour Party.

The imperialist war revealed only too clearly that the labour bureaucracy and the labour aristocracy had in the preceding period of capitalist development succeeded in passing through a profound petty bourgeois degeneration, in the sense of a vital exhaustion of all their mental reserves. But the petty bourgeoisie preserves the *semblance* of independence until the first clash. With one blow the war lay bare and strengthened the political dependence of the petty bourgeoisie on the great and greater bourgeoisie.

Social imperialism was one form of that dependence within the Labour Movement. But centralism, in so far as it was preserved or regenerated during the war period and after, was the expression of the terror of the petty bourgeoisie among the labour bureaucrats before a complete, and what is more important, an open enslavement to imperialism. German social democracy, which for many years, and even in the time of Bebel, carried out an essentially centralist policy, as a result of its very power could not retain this position in war-time: it had then either to be against the war, in other words, to take an essentially revolutionary course, or in favour of the war, in other words, to go over openly to the camp of the bourgeoisie. The British Independent Labour Party, as a propagandist organisation within the working class, was able not only to preserve, but even temporarily to strengthen, its centralist features during the war, "absolving itself of all responsibility," occupying itself with platonic protests, pacifist proclamations, not carrying any one of its ideas to its logical conclusion, and not causing any serious difficulties to the warring State. The opposition of the Independents in Germany, who also "absolved themselves of responsibility," while not hindering Scheidemann and Ebert from placing all the forces of the workers' organisations at the service of warring capital, was also of a centralist character.

In Britain after the war there was a unique combination of social-imperialist and centralist tendencies in the Labour Movement. The Independent Labour Party, as we have already said, could not have been better adapted to the rôle of an irresponsible centrist opposition, which criticises, but does not do any great harm to, the rulers. However, it was the fate of the Independents in a short time to become a political force, and this at the same moment changed their rôle and their features.

The Independents became a force owing to the intersection of two causes: First, because history faced the working class with the necessity of creating its own party; and secondly, because the war and the post-war period, having aroused the many-millioned masses, formed at first a favourable medium for the propagation of the idea of labour pacifism and reformism. It goes without saying that there were not a few democratic-pacifist illusions in the heads of the British workers even before the war. The difference none the less was colossal; in the past the British proletarian, in so far as he took part in political life, linked his democratic pacifist illusions—especially during the course of the second half of the nineteenth century—with the activity of the Liberal Party. But the latter "did not justify" these hopes, and lost the confidence of the workers. A separate Labour Party grew up as an invaluable historic achievement, from which nothing can ever detract. But one must clearly realise that the working masses are more disillusioned with the good will of Liberalism than with the democratic-pacifist methods of settling the social problem, the more so as new generations, fresh millions are being for the first time attracted to politics. They have transferred their hopes and illusions to the Labour Party. It is because of this, and only because of this, that the Independents have obtained the possibility of heading it. Beneath the democratic-pacifist illusions of the working masses *lies their awakened class will, a profound dissatisfaction with their situation, a readiness to support their demands by all the means that circumstances demand*. But it is possible for the working class to build up a party from those ideological and personal directing elements which have been prepared by all the previous development of the country, by all its theoretical and political culture. Here, speaking broadly, is the source of the great influence of the petty bourgeois intelligentsia, including in these, of course, the labour aristocracy and bureaucrats. The formation of a British Labour Party became a necessity just because a profound movement to the left took place in the working masses. The political formulation of this movement fell to the lot of those representatives of helpless Conservative-Protestant pacifism who were to hand. But in transferring their staff on to the groundwork of some millions of organised workers, the Independents could not remain themselves—in other words, they could not simply put their centristic stamp on the party of the proletariat. Having dropped into the leadership of a party composed of millions of workers, they could no longer confine themselves to centralist reservations and pacifist passivism. They had first, in the quality of a responsible opposition, and then, in the capacity of a government, to answer either "yes" or "no" to the most severe questions of State existence. From the moment that centrism became a political force, it was compelled to pass beyond the confines of centrism, in other words, it had either to draw revolutionary conclusions from its opposition to the imperialist State, or openly to enter its service. It goes without saying that the latter was what happened. The pacifist MacDonald began to build cruisers, to cast Indians and Egyptians into prison, to operate in the realm of diplomacy with the aid of false documents. Having become a political force, centrism as centrism became a nullity. The profound movement of the British working class *to the left*, which brought MacDonald's party to government with unexpected speed, conditioned the latter's manifest swing to the right. Such is the link between yesterday and to-day, and that is the reason why a small Independent Labour Party looks with bitter lack of comprehension on its successes and tries to pretend to be centrist.

The practical programme of the British Labour Party, directed by the Independents, has an essentially Liberal character, and represents, especially in its external policy, a belated refrain of the Gladstonian impotence. Gladstone was "compelled" to seize Egypt in a similar fashion to the way in which MacDonald was "compelled" to build cruisers. Beaconsfield reflected the imperialistic needs of capital more faithfully than Gladstone. Free Trade will now no longer settle a single question. The refusal to fortify Singapore is ridiculous from the point of view of the whole system of British imperialism. Singapore is the key to two oceans. Whoever desires to retain the colonies, in other words, to continue the policy of imperialist rapacity, must have that key in his own hands. MacDonald remains on capitalist ground, but makes cowardly alterations in it, which settle nothing, save from nothing, but increase all the difficulties and dangers.

On the question of the fate of British industry there is no real difference in the policy of the three parties. The main feature of this policy is a confusion born of dread of an upheaval. All three parties are conservative and fear industrial conflicts more than anything else. A Conservative Parliament refuses to grant the establishment of a living wage to the miners. The representatives elected by the miners say that the conduct of Parliament is a "direct incitement to revolutionary action," although not one of them seriously contemplates revolutionary action. The capitalists propose to the workers that they should together investigate the condition of the mining industry, hoping to demonstrate what has no need of demonstration, namely, that under the present system in the mining industry, disorganised as it is by private ownership, coal production is expensive even with a low scale of wages. The Conservative and Liberal Press see salvation in the investigation, the workers' leaders take the same attitude. All are afraid of strikes, which may have the effect of strengthening the predominance of foreign competition. Meanwhile, if it is at all possible to carry through some kind of nationalisation of industry under capitalism, it will be achieved only by means of huge strike pressure from the side of the workers. By paralysing the working masses through the trade unions, the leaders support the process of economic stagnation and decomposition.

One of those in the Labour Party membership who are quite definitely reactionary, Dr. Haden Guest, a Chauvinist, militarist, and Protectionist, pitilessly jeered in Parliament at the line taken by his own party in the question of Free Trade and Protection: MacDonald's position, according to Guest, has a purely negative character, and does not indicate any way out of the economic impasse. In actuality, the moribund character of Free Trade is absolutely obvious; for the dissolution of the Free Trade doctrine is signified by the dissolution of the Liberal Party. But just as little may Britain seek a way out in protection. For a young, just developing capitalist country protectionism may be an inevitable and progressive stage of development. But for an older industrial country, the industry of which was calculated for a world market and was characterised by aggression and conquest, the transfer to Protection is an historic testimony to the beginning of the process of mortification, and signifies in practice the support of one sphere of industry less capable of life in the given world situation at the expense of another section of the same British industry, more adapted to the conditions of the world or internal market. To the programme of old-fashioned protectionism of Baldwin's party may be opposed not the old-fashioned, moribund Free Trade doctrine in the least, but only a practical programme of socialist transformation. But in order to set about this programme it is necessary as a preliminary to cleanse the party both from the reactionary Protectionists such as Guest, and from reactionary Free Traders such as MacDonald.

From which side and in what manner can there be a change in the policy of the Labour Party, a change which is inconceivable without a radical change of leadership?

As the absolute majority on the Executive Committee and in the other more important institutions of the British Labour Party belongs to the Independent Labour Party, the latter forms a governing faction in the Labour Party. It is to the point to mention that this system of mutual relationships within the British Labour Movement provides extraordinarily valuable material on the question of the "dictatorship of a minority," for in just such terms, i.e. as a dictatorship of a minority, do the leaders of the British party define the rôle of the Communist Party in the Soviet Republic. We see, however, how the Independent Labour Party, numbering 30,000 members, obtains a controlling position in an organisation based through the trade unions on millions of members. But this organisation, i.e. the Labour Party, thanks to the numbers and rôle of the British proletariat, comes to government. Thus, a most insignificant minority of 30,000 members gets into its hands the government of a country numbering 40 millions of population and commanding hundreds of millions. The most actual "democracy" leads consequently to the party dictatorship of a minority. True, the "dictatorship" of the Independent Labour Party is not worth a dead cat in the class sense, but that is quite another question. If, however, a party of 30,000 members, without a revolutionary programme, without a militant temper, without serious traditions, by means of an amorphous Labour Party based on trade unions, can come to office, using the methods of bourgeois democracy, why do these gentlemen wax so indignant or seem so astonished when a Communist Party, both theoretically and practically tempered, with decades of heroic struggle at the head of the working-class masses in the past, a party numbering hundreds of thousands of members, comes to power, basing itself on the mass organisation of workers and peasants? In any case, the coming to power of the Independent Labour Party is immeasurably less deeply grounded and rooted than was the coming to power of the Communist Party in Russia.

But the dizzy career of the Independent Labour Party has interest not only from the aspect of polemic against judgments on the dictatorship of a Communist minority. It is immeasurably more important to evaluate the quick uplifting of the Independents from the aspect of the future destiny of the British Communist Party. Certain conclusions in this regard demand to be drawn.

The Independent Labour Party, born in a petty

bourgeois *milieu* and in its feelings and sympathies close to the *milieu* of the trade union bureaucracy, quite naturally together with it headed the Labour Party, when the masses by their pressure compelled their secretariats to create the latter. None the less, the Independent Labour Party, by its fantastic progress, its political methods, and by all its rôle, prepares and clears the ground—for the Communist Party. In the course of a decade the Independent Labour Party has only gathered altogether 30,000 members. But when a profound change in the international situation and in the internal structure of British society gave birth to the Labour Party, suddenly was revealed an unexpected demand for the leadership of the Independents. This same movement in political development prepares at the next stage a still more powerful "demand" for Communism. At the present moment the Communist Party is numerically very small. At the last elections it obtained altogether only 50,000 votes, a number which in comparison with the $5\frac{1}{2}$ million votes of the Labour Party, can give a crushing impression, if the logic of Britain's political development is not borne in mind. To think that the Communists will in the course of a decade grow step by step, acquiring at each new parliamentary election some tens or hundreds of thousands of fresh votes, would be to present its future in a radically false light. Of course, for the period of a certain comparatively long period Communism will develop comparatively slowly, but after that an inevitable change will take place: *The Communist Party will take that place in relation to the Labour Party which at present is occupied by the Independent Labour Party.*

What is necessary in order to achieve this? The general answer is absolutely clear. The Independent

Labour Party has achieved its unprecedented rise because it assisted the working class to form a third, i.e. their own, party. The last elections show what enthusiasm the British workers display for the instrument created by them. But a party is not an end in itself. From it the workers expect action and results. The British Labour Party grew up almost in a moment as a party, making direct pretensions to government, and having already succeeded in habituating itself to government. Despite the profoundly discrediting nature of the first "labour" Government, the party gained over a million fresh votes at the election. Within the party, however, was formed the so-called left wing, amorphous, spineless, incapable of any independent future. But the very fact of the development of opposition testifies to the growth of demand in the masses and of a parallel access of caution in the upper ranks of the party. Some small consideration of the nature of the MacDonalds, Thomases, Clyneses, and Snowdens, and all the others, is sufficient to conceive how catastrophically will grow the inconsistencies between the demands of the masses and the stupid conservatism of the directing groups of the Labour Party, especially in the event of their coming again to office.

In outlining this perspective, we start from the hypothesis that the present international and internal situation of British capitalism will not only not improve, but on the contrary will continue to get worse. If this prognostication were to prove incorrect, if the British bourgeoisie were to succeed in strengthening the empire, in recovering for itself its former position on the world market, in uplifting industry, in giving work to the unemployed, in raising the workers' wages, then the political development would take on an intelligible turn: the aristocratic conservatism of the trade unions would again be strengthened, the Labour Party would fall into a decline, within it its right wing would be strengthened, under which circumstances the latter would draw closer to Liberalism, which in turn would experience a certain influx of vital forces. But there is not the least foundation for such a prognostication. On the contrary, whatever may happen to be the particular variation of the economic and political position, everything points to the further intensification and deepening of those difficulties through which Britain is at present passing, and therefore to a further quickening of the tempo of her revolutionary development. But under those conditions the coming to power of the Labour Party in one of the earliest stages is extremely probable, and then a conflict between the working class and the Fabian group at present heading it will be seen to be absolutely unavoidable.

The present rôle of the Independents arises out of the fact that their path has intersected with that of the proletariat. But this by no means signifies that these roads have united once for all. The quick growth of influence of the Independents is only the reflection of the exceptional strength of the working-class pressure; but that very pressure, conditioned by the whole situation, will bring the workers into conflict with the Independent leaders. In the measure that this takes place the revolutionary qualities of the British Communist Party will, assuming, of course, a correct policy, result in a mass-membership.

There would seem to be some analogy between the destinies of the Communist and of the Independent Labour Parties. Both of them have for a long time existed rather as propagandist bodies than as parties of the working class. Then, with a profound break in the historic development of Britain, the Independent Labour Party took the lead of the proletariat. After a certain interval the Communist Party will, we think, be raised in a similar fashion.[1] The path of its development will at a certain point unite with the great historic road of the British proletariat. However, this union will take place in quite a different fashion from that of the Independent Labour Party. For the latter the connecting-link was the bureaucracy of the trade unions. The Independents can lead the Labour Party so long as the professional bureaucracy weakens, neutralises, and distorts the independent class pressure of the proletariat. But the Communist Party, on the contrary, can only come to the head of the working class in the measure that the latter comes into irreconcilable antagonism with the conservative bureaucracy in the trade unions and in the Labour Party. The Communist Party can prepare for the rôle of leadership only by a relentless criticism of all the directing personnel of the British Labour Movement, only by a day in and day out denunciation of its conservative, anti-proletarian, imperialistic, monarchistic, lackey-like rôle in all spheres of social life and of the class movement.

The left wing of the Labour Party represents an attempt at the resurrection of centrism within the social-imperialist party of MacDonald. It thus reflects the agitation of a part of the labour bureaucracy for a connection with the leftward moving masses. It would be a monstrous illusion to think

[1] It goes without saying that this kind of forecast is of a contingent and general character, and in no case should it be identified with astronomical forecasts of eclipses of the moon or the sun. The actual course of development is always inevitably more complicated than a diagrammatic forecast.

that these left elements of the old school are capable of heading the revolutionary movement of the British proletariat and its struggle for power. In themselves they represent a completed formation. They have only a very limited elasticity, their leftism is opportunist throughout. They will not lead and they are not capable of leading the masses to the struggle. Within the bounds of their reformistic limitations they are reviving the old irresponsible centralism, not hindering but rather helping MacDonald to carry the responsibility for leadership of the party, and in certain cases for the destiny of the British Empire.

This picture could not have been better revealed than it was at the Gloucester Conference of the Independent Labour Party (Easter 1925). While grumbling against MacDonald, the Independents gave their approval to the so-called "activity" of the Labour Government by 398 votes to 139. But even the opposition could allow themselves the luxury of disapproval only because the majority was assured to MacDonald. The dissatisfaction of the lefts with MacDonald is the dissatisfaction of centrism with itself. It is not possible to improve the policy of MacDonald by mosaic corrections. If centrism comes to power, it will inevitably carry on a MacDonaldite, in other words a capitalist, policy. The MacDonald method can be seriously opposed only by the method of the socialist dictatorship of the proletariat. It would be the greatest of illusions to think that the party of the Independents is capable of developing into a revolutionary party of the proletariat. The Fabians must be eliminated, "removed from their positions." This can be achieved only by the way of an irreconcilable struggle with the centrism of the Independents.

The more clearly and sharply the question of the

conquest of power emerges, the more will the Independent Labour Party endeavour to slide out of answering, supplanting the basic revolutionary problem by bureaucratic imaginings on the question of the best parliamentary and financial methods of nationalising industry. One of the committees of the Independent Labour Party came to the conclusion that the purchase of the land, workshops, and factories is to be preferred to their confiscation, since in Britain, according to the presentiment of the committee, nationalisation will take place gradually, in Baldwin fashion, step by step, and it would be "unjust" to deprive one group of capitalists of their receipts while another group was still receiving interest on its capital. "It would be another matter," the report of the committee reads (we quote from its exposition in *The Times*), "if Socialism were to come not gradually, but suddenly, as the result of a catastrophic revolution: then the arguments against confiscation would lose most of their force." "But we," continues the report, "do not think that this contingency is likely to arise, *and we do not feel called upon* to discuss it in the present report." Broadly speaking, there is no ground for rejection on principle of the purchase of the land, factories, and workshops. But unfortunately, however, the political and the financial possibilities of such an operation will never fall together. The state of finances of the North American Republic would render the purchasing operation completely possible. But in America the question itself is not a practical issue, and there is no party as yet which could put it forward seriously. And by the time such a party appears the economic position of the United States will necessarily have undergone an extremely severe alteration. In Britain, on the contrary, the question of nationalisation is on the point of decision, as being a question of the salvation of British economic life. But the state of the national finances is such that the possibility of buying out seems more than doubtful. However, the financial side of the question is only a secondary matter. The chief task is the creation of the political prerequisites of nationalisation, and whether with purchase or without is a matter of indifference. In the last resort it is a question of the life or death of the bourgeoisie. Therefore, revolution is inevitable just because the bourgeoisie will never allow itself to be choked by means of Fabian banking operations. Bourgeois society, in its present condition, will not accept even a partial nationalisation except by circumscribing it with such conditions as must render the successful carrying through of the measures extremely difficult, and must discredit the principle of nationalisation and with it the Labour Party. But to any really bold attempt at nationalisation, even though it be only partial, the bourgeoisie will react as a class. Other spheres of industry will resort to lockouts, to sabotage, to a boycott of the nationalised sections—in other words, will carry on a struggle for life or death, and to the death. However cautious the initial approach may be, the task will just as surely come to be the necessity of smashing the opposition of the exploiters. When the Fabians inform us that they do not feel themselves "called upon" to consider this "contingency," we have to say that these gentlemen have made a complete mistake as to their calling. It is extremely possible that those of them who are most men of affairs will be of service in this or that department of the future workers' state, where they will be occupied with the calculation of separate elements of a socialist balance-sheet. But they will never be of any value so long as the question is how to set up the workers' state—in other words, the basic prerequisite of socialist economy.

In one of his weekly surveys in the *Daily Herald* (April 4, 1925), by a slip of the pen, MacDonald gave vent to some realistic remarks. "The situation of parties in our day," he said, "is such that the struggle will become continually more defined and strong. The Conservative Party will struggle to the death, and the more threatening becomes the government of the Labour Party, the more monstrous will be the pressure of its reactionary members." That is absolutely correct. The more immediate the danger of the Labour Party coming to power becomes, the stronger will become the influence in the Conservative Party of such people as Curzon. (Not for nothing did MacDonald call him the "pattern" for future men of affairs.) It would seem that for once the estimate of the prospect made by MacDonald was correct. But in actuality the leader of the Labour Party does not himself understand the significance and weight of his words. The appeal to the fact that the Conservatives will fight to the death, and the farther they go the more violent will be their struggle, was of value to him only in order that he might prove the inexpediency of inter-party parliamentary committees. But in its essentials the forecast made by MacDonald tells not only against inter-party parliamentary committees, but also against the possibility of settling the whole present social crisis by parliamentary methods. "The Conservative Party will fight to the death." Correct! But that means that the Labour Party can beat it only in the event that it excels the Conservative Party in its determination in the struggle. It is not a question of the rivalry of two parties, but of the fate of two classes. But when two classes struggle to the death, the question is never decided by counting votes. Never has that been the case at any time in history. And it never will be the case in history so long as classes exist.

However, the question is not of the general philosophy of MacDonald, and not of his individual fortunate slips of the tongue—in other words, not of what he desires, but of what he does and to what his activities lead. If the question be approached from this end, it is seen that in all its work the MacDonald party is preparing the way for a gigantic development and strengthening in the British proletarian revolution. It is the very party of MacDonald that is strengthening the confidence of the bourgeoisie and at the same time stretches the endurance of the proletariat to its last limits. And just about when that patience gives out, the proletariat, having resorted to their fists, will come up against the bourgeoisie face to face, the bourgeoisie that MacDonald's party has only strengthened in the consciousness of its omnipotence. The longer the Fabians restrain the revolutionary development of Britain, the more threatening and raging will be the explosion.

The British bourgeoisie has been brought up on ruthlessness. The conditions of island existence, the moral philosophy of Calvinism, colonial practices, and national arrogance have led them along that road. Britain to-day is being more and more relegated to a back place. The British bourgeoisie, compelled to humiliate itself before America, yields place, manœuvres, and hangs on, filled with a spirit of the greatest obduracy, which will be displayed in dangerous forms in a civil war. So the bourgeois rabble of France, broken in the war with the Prussians, revenged itself on the

Communards; so the officerdom of the battered Hohenzollern army revenged itself on the German workers.

All that cold cruelty which the rulers of Britain display towards the Indians, Egyptians, and Irish, and which has the semblance of racial arrogance, will in the event of a civil war reveal its class character and will show itself to be directed against the proletariat.

On the other hand, the revolution will inevitably arouse a tremendous fervour in the British working class, that fervour which has been so artificially restrained and repressed with the aid of social training, the Church, the Press, and has been drawn off into artificial channels with the aid of boxing, football, racing, and other forms of sport.

The concrete course of the struggle, its duration, and its issue, will entirely depend on the internal and, especially, on the international conditions prevailing at the moment when it develops. In the decisive struggle against the proletariat the British bourgeoisie will avail themselves of the most powerful support of the bourgeoisie of the United States, while the working class will base itself mainly on the working class of Europe and the oppressed peoples of the British Colonies. The nature of the British Empire will inevitably give this gigantic struggle an international scale. It will be one of the greatest dramas in the world's history. In this struggle the destiny of the British proletariat will be bound up with the fate of all humanity. The whole world circumstance and rôle of the British proletariat in industry and in society will ensure its victory—given the conditions of a correct and determined revolutionary leadership. The Communist Party must develop and come to power, as the party of proletarian dictatorship. There are no ways round the difficulty. Whoever believes and preaches that there is can only delude the British workers. That is the main conclusion to be drawn from our analysis.

INDEX